Birth of a Movement

BIRTH OF A MOVEMENT

Black Lives Matter and the Catholic Church

Olga M. Segura

ORBIS BOOKS
Maryknoll, New York 10545

Founded in 1970, Orbis Books endeavors to publish works that enlighten the mind, nourish the spirit, and challenge the conscience. The publishing arm of the Maryknoll Fathers and Brothers, Orbis seeks to explore the global dimensions of the Christian faith and mission, to invite dialogue with diverse cultures and religious traditions, and to serve the cause of reconciliation and peace. The books published reflect the views of their authors and do not represent the official position of the Maryknoll Society. To learn more about Orbis Books, please visit our website at www.orbisbooks.com.

Library of Congress Cataloging-in-Publication Data

Names: Segura, Olga M., author.
Title: Birth of a movement : Black lives matter and the Catholic Church / Olga M. Segura.
Description: Maryknoll, New York : Orbis Books, [2021] | Includes bibliographical references and index. | Summary: "Birth of a Movement tells the story of the Black Lives Matter movement through a Christian lens. Readers will gain a deeper understanding of the movement and why it can help the church, and the country, move closer to racial equality. Readers will understand why Black Lives Matter is a truly "Christ-like movement.""— Provided by publisher.
Identifiers: LCCN 2020036197 (print) | LCCN 2020036198 (ebook) | ISBN 9781626984202 (print) | ISBN 9781608338832 (ebook)
Subjects: LCSH: Catholic Church—United States. | Race relations—Religious aspects—Catholic Church. | Black lives matter movement.
Classification: LCC BX1407.N4 S44 2021 (print) | LCC BX1407.N4 (ebook) |
    DDC 261.8/32808996073—dc23
LC record available at https://lccn.loc.gov/2020036197
LC ebook record available at https://lccn.loc.gov/2020036198

para Francisca y Julio Segura

Contents

Foreword

The Call Is Coming from Inside the House

Tia Noelle Pratt, PhD

I've been researching and writing about Black Catholics and systemic racism in the Catholic Church for over twenty years. In my career, I've never seen issues of racism in the church and the broader society dovetail in the way they have in 2020. This is why Olga M. Segura has gifted us with an urgent, necessary book. *Birth of a Movement: Black Lives Matter and the Catholic Church* is simultaneously a response to the period of history we are all living in and the call to action the church desperately needs to answer to survive.

The birth of the Catholic Church in the United States is comingled with the slave trade in North America. As Segura rightly notes, it was the Catholic Church that introduced chattel slavery to what is now the United States. If the Catholic Church in the United States will ever close the gulf between the values it extols and the values it practices, the work must begin with a reckoning of this truth and all that it has wrought. Olga Segura offers us a blueprint for this task.

George Floyd's murder in Minneapolis, Minnesota, in May 2020, initiated a global reckoning around systemic racism that was long overdue. In the months since, I have made the expression "The Call Is Coming from Inside the House" a focal point of my lectures and media interviews. We cannot dismiss this call to action as something that is relevant only to people and places far removed from ourselves. In whatever space we live, work, and worship, we must respond to this page-turner moment in history through direct, concrete action. The Roman Catholic Church is not immune to this call and must not continue to intentionally ignore an issue that has rotted the church from the inside for hundreds of years.

Part call to action, part spiritual memoir, part exegesis on church teachings, *Birth of a Movement* deftly interweaves the origins and purpose of the Black Lives Matter (BLM) movement with the Catholic Church and the church's failure to support Blacks—whether they are Catholic or not. Those who erroneously believe that the BLM movement and church teachings are in conflict need not look any further than the pages of this book to see the myriad ways the two intersect. In fact, by embracing the values of BLM, Catholicism can begin to embody the values it preaches but often fails to practice.

The way Segura moves between the individual and organizational levels of analysis greatly benefits those who don't do that in their own thinking but need to. As part of her blueprint for building a better church—and, by extension, a better world—Segura calls on the United States Conference of Catholic Bishops (USCCB) to write a pastoral letter focused "on the harm that has been done," one that will allow our church leaders to "apologize for how the institutional church has been and continues to be complicit in white supremacy." In this way, "our church leaders can apologize for the pain inflicted on our communities, from the days of chattel slavery to the police murders of the twenty-first century."

There are some, including bishops, who will read this only with a mindset of individual, or personal-level, racism and insist that since current bishops don't own slaves, burn crosses on lawns, or murder Black people in the street, there is no reason to apologize. That attitude betrays the limitations of hovering at the mindset of personal-level racism and not expanding one's imagination and thinking to the level of racial justice and anti-racism. Continuing to live at that level allows white Catholics to persist with the erroneous supposition that none of this has anything to do with them. In fact, it has *everything* to do with them! It is hundreds of years past the time to move beyond this stagnant level of thinking. The first step in making that happen is acknowledging the way twenty-first-century white Catholics continue to benefit from the system their white Catholic fore-bears birthed into existence hundreds of years ago.

Those who are not willing to do even that must stop blanketing their lawns and social media accounts with performative platitudes because it's just a waste of time. Approximately 40 percent of Catholics in the United States are Black, Latino, Asian-American, and Native American. This number is higher among younger Catholics. An institution cannot continue to marginalize people—especially in the ways in which the church, as Segura elucidates, has marginalized Black people—and still expect those same people to remain active in the institution. To think otherwise is at best disingenuous and at most ludicrous. Yet, this brings us to the question Segura grapples with in this book and that I've been asked many times in my own work: "How do Black people remain Catholic through all of this?" This is a question, frankly, that only white Catholics ask because belonging to an institution that wasn't created for, and continues to exist for, their benefit is unfathomable to them. I answer this question by invoking my late great-uncle, Calvin Aguillard, Sr.

Uncle Calvin was a lifelong resident of New Orleans and was known in the city's rich, Black Catholic community for his activism and commitment to the church. While visiting with him close to twenty years ago, I began telling him about my research that focuses on systemic racism in the Catholic Church and how that racism impacted Black Catholics. He, in turn, told me about his work in his community and said, "Baby, this is *my* church, too, and I'm not going to let them mess it up!" In all the years since, that is the only answer I give because it is the only answer I need.

As I write this on September 23, 2020, Kentucky's attorney general has just announced there will be no charges in the death of Breonna Taylor. The only charges filed relate to the three shots—the three counts of "wanton endangerment"—that were fired into her neighbor's apartment. The Commonwealth of Kentucky will not demand any accountability directly related to Breonna Taylor's death. Kentucky has decided that Breonna Taylor's life did not matter. It is for her and so many others, including ourselves, that we say Black Lives Matter. We must continue to proclaim this until we have systems that are structured accordingly.

We still have a Catholic Church that issues pastoral letters that condemn personal racism but does not even acknowledge systemic racism. Doing so would first require the church to account for its own systemic racism. For the church to even acknowledge its systemic racism, the overwhelmingly white bishops who make up the USCCB would have to renounce the white supremacy which they benefit from and which is the source of their power in the Catholic Church in the United States. Until that happens, we must—and we will—continue to assert that Black Lives Matter, Black Catholic Lives Matter, and that the Call Is Coming from Inside the House.

Acknowledgments

Enoch, this book would not be possible without you. You were the first person to help me publicly call myself a writer. You have believed in me and challenged me since the first day we met. Your faith is one of the strongest I have seen. Thank you for talking theology with me while we played Trouble. Thank you for encouraging me not to be afraid of Scripture and to believe in my own relationship with Christ. For all the meals you cooked, the chores you handled alone while I huddled over my laptop, for all the times you listened as I talked my chapters and ideas out loud, and for supporting me during every moment of anxiety, fear, or doubt. Thank you for loving me, for helping me grow in my faith, and for believing in me. I love you.

Thank you to my parents, Francisca and Julio, who left the Dominican Republic in pursuit of a better life. You sacrificed everything for the people you loved. Every one of us—aunts, uncles, cousins—who have arrived in this country are here because of you. Thank you for raising us, for educating us, for encouraging us to step outside our comfort zone, and most importantly, thank you for encouraging us to dream. We are storytellers because you gave us our voices.

Thank you to my sister, Pamela. All of my favorite memories involve you, from playing office, to performing our favorite songs, to helping me write my first play featuring Ja Rule and Ashanti. You are my best friend, my sister. You are the most brilliant writer I know. I cannot wait for you to write your story. You continue to inspire me with your strength, your sense of self, and your commitment to justice. Toni Morrison said, "A sister can be seen as someone who is both ourselves and very much not ourselves—a special kind of double." Without you, there would be no me.

Thank you to my aunt, Rosa. Thank you for helping me become the professional woman I am today. Thank you for holding me when I cried, especially that one time in Central Park; for the dinners when you listened to me anxiously try to figure out my place in this world. Thank you for listening, for believing, and for all the free lunches and dinners and drinks.

To Estefany, thank you for always holding me accountable and for supporting me. To Will and Brian, thank you for all the Google Chat conversations; for pushing me to ask for more at work; and for always hyping me up. TEAM HAM for life. To Eloise Blondiau, thank you for listening to my rants, reading my drafts, and for showing me what it means to empower women in the workplace. To James Martin, thank you for believing in my Catholic voice, for sharing my work, and, most importantly, for helping me get my first book deal. And finally, thank you to America Media for giving me the space to cultivate my voice and expertise.

Introduction

When signing the contract for this book in 2019, my intention at the time was to provide Catholics with a history of the Black Lives Matter movement, including both its successes and its criticisms. I knew people had misconceptions of the movement, including the belief that all the founders were irreligious or had no understanding of faith. Throughout my years of reporting, critics told me that the movement was not concerned with human dignity (false); the movement was violent (false); and that the founders have all publicly identified as atheists and completely denigrate religion whenever possible (false). One male critic even sent me a Twitter direct message explaining that I "clearly misunderstood both Catholicism and the terrorist group that was the BLM," because the movement's "rejection of capitalism was dangerous and antithetical to Christianity." I never responded, yet this particular fallacy is one that I have often heard, and which, when used by Catholics, demonstrates how little they know about its founders—Alicia Garza, Patrisse Cullors, and Opal Tometi—and Pope Francis.

I envisioned a book that would reject such ideas and gently challenge our white bishops to grapple with the movement's mission. I wanted the body of all male, almost all white, bishops to internalize the movement's beliefs and imagined white Christians reading this book and feeling inspired to dismantle the white supremacy within our church—one that seems as fundamental to the American church as the Eucharist is integral to our faith. This book, I thought at the time, could be the Catholic version of Ibram X. Kendi's *How to Be an Antiracist*; but then 2020 happened.

For the first time since the terrorist attacks of September 11, 2001, the city that raised me—one that was always noisy, crowded, and alert—shut down. The first COVID-19 case in the United States was confirmed in January; by the end of that month, the Trump administration had closed our nation's borders to people traveling from China. By March, the New York Department of Education, which oversees the largest school district in the United States, closed all public schools; the subway system shut down; companies across all industries transitioned to remote work; stores closed; restaurants went out of business; and the theater district, Broadway, closed. People were furloughed and lost jobs. Mothers, for a brief time, gave birth in hospitals without partners or a support system, just the medical staff. By May, the state had the largest number of confirmed cases and deaths. The sheer number of people who died daily overburdened hospitals; many did not have enough beds, ventilators, or staff. One of the richest cities in the world was clearly struggling with the global pandemic. By June 1, thousands of New Yorkers were dead; many more had lost jobs and health insurance; and a large percentage could not afford their month's rent. I struggled to understand why the U.S. government was willing to let so many people from my communities die; why working class Americans were only given a single $1,200 ($2,400 for families), while billionaires like Jeff Bezos grew richer during a global pandemic that was robbing Blacks and Latinos of their lives.

In April, my father became ill. At first, we thought it was just a regular cold, but steadily his symptoms grew worse. He slept for days at a time, had a cough and fever, and his body ached. When my father tried to get tested, he was told that his symptoms were not serious enough. My father, and all of us, accepted this. "There were people who literally couldn't breathe when I went to the hospital—I felt bad even going," he told us. However, this was not an anomaly. Across the United States, Black women, men, and children were being denied testing by a medical system that was created by white doctors, who had experimented on Black bodies without consent and anesthetics. Across the country, ZIP Codes with more money—areas that were predominantly white—disproportionately received access to testing. By April, studies confirmed that Blacks and Latinos were dying at almost three times the rate of white citizens. Black and Brown families were being devastated, while our political leaders continued to publicly spar with the president. The first COVID-19 death in New York happened in March; by July, more than thirty thousand New Yorkers were dead.

As the global pandemic ravaged Black and Latino communities, police officers across the country were harassing and killing Americans. In New York, the police used the enforcement of social distancing to justify their disproportionate harassment of Black and Brown citizens. In the first half of 2020 alone, police officers killed more than five hundred Americans, including twenty-eight-year-old Xavier Jaime Rovie, who was shot and killed in Phoenix, Arizona; seventy-five-year-old John Daniel Dixon, who was shot and killed in DeKalb County, Georgia; fifty-five-year-old Deanne Marie Owsianiak, who was killed in Ormond Beach, Florida; forty-two-year-old Charity Tome, who was shot and killed in Myerstown, Pennsylvania; twenty-five-year-old Catherine Gomez, who was killed in Long Beach, California; twenty-two-year-old Heba Momtaz Al-Azhari, who was shot and killed in Temple Terrace, Florida; eighteen-year-old Andres Guardado, who was killed in Los Angeles, California; seventeen-year-old Vincent Demario Truitt, who was shot and killed in Cobb County, Georgia; and twenty-two-year-old Hannah R. Fizer, who was killed in Sedalia, Missouri. Since 2015, police officers across the country have killed more than five thousand Americans. I understood, in a way I never had before, the legal power law enforcement is given to harass, assault, and murder, with nearly universal impunity. By the summer, antipolice protests erupted across the United States following the murders of Breonna Taylor and George Floyd. Black women, men, and children filled American streets demanding justice; cries that have existed since the days of the first antislavery rebellion. Alongside them, white men, women, and children, including Catholic clergy, were publicly calling for an end to murder by police. In June, I attended a protest—my first in years. The message from the marchers, a majority of whom carried Puerto Rican and Dominican flags, was clear: there could be no equality in a world with policing. A liberated world meant abolishing law enforcement and the prison industrial complex that belonged to it.

The antiracism rebellion and the COVID-19 global pandemic politicized me, and countless others, unexpectedly. This book, in turn, was reimagined as a call to white Catholics, both lay and clergy, to work actively and consistently to abolish every system that oppresses, rapes, and murders Black women, men, and children.

Birth of a Movement is structured to include histories of the Black Lives Matter movement and the church's history with white supremacy. We discuss the Catholic perspective, the birth of modern American policing, abolition, racial capitalism, reparations, and church leadership. This book is also, to borrow Garza's words, my love letter to the women—both within and outside of the church—who have shaped my politics and Catholic identity. These women include Shannen Dee Williams, whose scholarship taught me about our church's active participation in chattel slavery and who guided my focus on citing, almost exclusively, Black women throughout the book; M. Shawn Copeland, whose work inspired me to consider, for the first time, the power of the resurrection and its role in the struggle toward Black liberation; Tia Noelle Pratt, a sociologist, creator of the "Black Catholic Syllabus," and writer of the foreword; and the founders of the Black Lives Matter movement, Garza, Cullors, and Tometi, who have given purpose to my life, faith, and career. The goal is to help Catholics, and all Christians, work toward a Christ-centered, Black liberation.

1

The March for Black Life

His is the story of a life cut tragically short, but it's also the story of a boy who in death became a symbol, a beacon, and a mirror in which a whole nation came to see its reflection. It's the story of a young life that at its seeming end was transfigured into something else.[1]

Sybrina Fulton and Tracy Martin met in December 1993. They married in June 1994, and on February 5, 1995, their son, Trayvon Martin, was born. He was a playful child, his parents write, one who loved football, music, and the outdoors. Growing up, Trayvon was adventurous, fearless. Tracy Martin writes that, when he was nine years old, Trayvon pulled him out of a fire and saved his life.[2] Whenever his mother was tired, Fulton, who co-authored the book, writes, Trayvon helped by doing chores around the house. He cooked, cleaned, shopped for groceries, and washed her car. Their son also loved aviation. Two years before his death, Trayvon attended a summer camp called Experience Aviation. The Jamaican-born American pilot

---

1. Sybrina Fulton and Tracy Martin, *Rest in Power: The Enduring Life of Trayvon Martin* (New York: Spiegel & Grau, 2017), x.
2. Ibid., 24.

Barrington Irving, who, at twenty-three, flew around the world alone, the first Black pilot to do so, created the camp in 2005 in Miami. At the camp, Irving uses planes to teach campers about engineering, math, and science. After a summer there when he was fifteen, Trayvon decided that he wanted to pursue a career in aviation. He was just a young boy, his parents write, going through all the regular ups and downs of adolescence with his entire life ahead of him.

On February 22, 2012, Trayvon went to stay with his father and his father's girlfriend, Brandy, in Sanford, Florida; he often split his time between Miami and Sanford after his parents divorced when he was five. Four days after arriving, Trayvon went to a 7-Eleven for Skittles and a can of Arizona iced tea. As he walked back home from the store, a neighborhood watchman named George Zimmerman, twenty-eight, followed the young boy. He eventually called the police to report Trayvon, a habit of Zimmerman's, because he claimed he was suspicious; he had previously reported at least four Black men to the police.[3] Zimmerman, who had never met Trayvon, formed an opinion that the young teenager was dangerous, based on nothing other than the white supremacist conditioning America had indoctrinated into him, one that told him that Trayvon, now seventeen years old, was a threat. After the adult accosted the teenager, the two got into an altercation. Zimmerman, who was allowed to legally own a firearm by the very government that taught him to fear Black children, shot and killed Trayvon. When he failed to return home the next day, February 27, his father called the police and reported his son missing. Within thirty minutes, detectives arrived at Martin's home to inform him that Trayvon had been murdered. In *Rest in Power*,

---

3. Yamiche Alcindor, "Trial Turns to Zimmerman's Neighborhood-Watch Role," *USA Today*, June 25, 2013, https://www.usatoday.com.

Tracy Martin describes, in heartbreaking details, the moment he identified his son's body:

> The picture burned a hole in my heart. It showed my seventeen-year-old son, as lifeless as a broken rag doll, on the wet grass, no more than a hundred yards from Brandy's townhouse. One of his legs was folded back on itself, and his eyes were slightly open, staring into a stranger's camera. The sweatshirt he wore beneath his hoodie was stained blackish red with blood from the gunshot wound to his heart.
>
> Trayvon was dead.[4]

Almost two months after killing Trayvon, Zimmerman was charged with second-degree murder. In Florida, however, a stand-your-ground state, Zimmerman had the right to own a weapon and defend himself; legally, his lawyer—and countless other Americans—argued, he had a right to kill. His trial began in June 2013. By July, more than a year after murdering Trayvon, Zimmerman was acquitted of all charges.

Following the acquittal, the activist and writer Alicia Garza, born in Los Angeles, California, wrote what she described to me in 2018 as a love letter to Black people on Facebook. Garza has been organizing since she was a teenager around issues such as access to birth control, gentrification, and anti-LGBTQIA violence. In 2009, Garza worked for People Organized to Win Employment Rights (POWER), an organization that fights for better housing, living wages, and immigrants' rights.[5] She currently directs special projects at the National Domestic Workers

---

4. Fulton and Martin, *Rest in Power*, 33.

5. "POWER (People Organized to Win Employment Rights)," Tenants Together, July 17, 2020, http://www.tenantstogether.org.

Alliance,[6] an advocacy group for U.S. domestic workers, and serves as the principal at Black Futures Lab,[7] an organization that works to get young Black people voting. She described her Facebook message as a call to fight for a world that genuinely valued Black women, men, and children outside of their contributions to the entertainment industry, a world where racist men such as Zimmerman were no longer allowed to view Black children as unworthy of human life and dignity. Her message was re-shared by Patrisse Cullors, a fellow Los Angeles–born artist and activist, with the hashtag #BlackLivesMatter. Garza, Cullors, and Arizona-born organizer Opal Tometi from Phoenix, three Black women, whose lives and careers are covered more fully in the next chapter, created the Black Lives Matter movement on social media.

The movement was originally conceived as a campaign to inspire a new generation of organizers. The founders used Twitter and Facebook to get people thinking and talking about the ways that Black life is devalued in America, from higher rates of incarceration for Black women and men to "adultification," which is defined by writer A. Rochaun Meadows-Fernandez as a form of racism where Black girls are perceived as more mature than other girls, and therefore, punished as adults.[8] The women wanted to inspire Americans, especially young people, to get involved in the struggle to eradicate anti-Black racism in the United States and, by extension, other countries. Since 2013, the hashtag has been shared more than thirty million times;[9]

6. National Domestic Workers Alliance, July 17, 2020, https://www.domesticworkers.org.

7. Black Futures Lab, July 17, 2020, https://blackfutureslab.org.

8. A. Rochaun Meadows-Fernandez, "Why Won't Society Let Black Girls Be Children?" *New York Times*, April 17, 2020, https://www.nytimes.com.

9. Monica Anderson et al., "An Analysis of #BlackLivesMatter

and by 2020, 60 percent of adult citizens surveyed in America, across ethnic and racial categories, expressed support for the Black Lives Matter movement.[10] In 2014, the founders, along with more than five hundred organizers from across the country, traveled to Ferguson, Missouri, following the killing of eighteen-year-old Michael Brown Jr., who was shot and killed by Darren Wilson, a white police officer, on August 9. Cullors and Darnell Moore, an activist and author of *No Ashes in the Fire: Coming of Age Black and Free in America*, organized the freedom ride, the movement's first in-person gathering. Every day of the ride, Garza said, they helped frontline organizers, many of whom were repeatedly tear-gassed and assaulted by riot police. For many Americans, the Ferguson uprising was the first time they learned of the Black Lives Matter movement.

In September, following the freedom ride, Cullors and Moore published an article in *The Guardian* listing the organization's policy demands at the time. They called for arresting Wilson, developing a network of organizations and activists to address the systemic racism in U.S. law enforcement, demilitarizing U.S. law enforcement, publishing the names of every police officer who killed a Black person, and defunding police budgets and redistributing those funds into Black communities as a step toward prison abolition.[11]

The mission of the movement, and of all the organizers

---

and Other Twitter Hashtags Related to Political or Social Issues," Pew Research Center, July 11, 2018, https://www.pewresearch.org.

10. Monica Anderson et al., "Amid Protests, Majorities across Racial and Ethnic Groups Express Support for the Black Lives Matter Movement," Pew Research Center, June 12, 2020, https://www.pewsocialtrends.org.

11. Patrisse Cullors and Darnell Moore, "5 Ways to Never Forget Ferguson—and Deliver Real Justice to Michael Brown," *The Guardian*, September 4, 2014, https://www.theguardian.com.

around the world who have internalized its message since 2013, was clear: "We work vigorously for freedom and justice for Black people and, by extension, all people."[12]

The Call to Write

My first report for *America* magazine on the movement was published in December 2014, following the acquittal of Daniel Pantaleo in the death of forty-three-year-old Eric Garner in Staten Island, New York, in July that same year. Like countless other Americans, I watched the footage of Garner's murder on Twitter. On July 17, police officers accosted Garner after they alleged that he was selling single, untaxed cigarettes. "I'm minding my business, officer," Garner is heard saying on the recorded footage of that day. "Please just leave me alone." Garner had his hands in the air when Pantaleo jumped onto his back and placed him into a chokehold. He pulled the Black father to the ground, never easing the pressure around Garner's neck. The forty-three-year-old repeatedly told officers that he could not breathe. Pantaleo released his chokehold and pushed the Black man's head into the concrete. "I can't breathe," Garner says at least five more times. Despite his pleas, Pantaleo, who represents an industry that has whitewashed men and women like him as pro-life heroes demonstrating "a higher standard of integrity than is generally expected of others,"[13] murdered a Black man in broad daylight. His death was lawful, according to the New York Police Department (NYPD) and many of its supporters, because not only was Garner selling cigarettes that deprived the

---

12. Black Lives Matter, "What We Believe," https://blacklives matter.com.

13. Cf. New York City Police Department, "Values," https:// www1.nyc.gov/site/nypd/about/about-nypd/mission.page.

state of money, he was also angry, resisting arrest, and a threat. Pantaleo only choked the Black father, many argued, because he feared for his own life. Garner's body, in other words, and the bodies of other Black women, men, and children could be endangered to save men who purportedly served and protected us. Like the system that created it, the NYPD ethos was clear: Black *lives* mattered less than *property*.

Pantaleo was tried, and in December 2014, he was acquitted. Almost five years after Garner's murder, James P. O'Neill, the NYPD commissioner from 2016 to 2019, stated that although Pantaleo used a move that was prohibited, he was correct to do so because Garner was illegally selling property that belonged to the state, sentiments that once again criminalized the murdered father years after his death The officer, who had an otherwise admirable career, the commissioner proclaimed, caused "multi-layered internal bruising and hemorrhaging that impaired Mr. Garner's physical condition and caused substantial pain and was a significant factor in triggering an asthma attack."[14] Pantaleo's actions, the NYPD ultimately concluded, went against the code of ethics police officers hold dear. In August 2019, five years after he killed Garner, Pantaleo was fired from the department.

In November 2014, just two weeks prior to Pantaleo's acquittal, I joined organizers in New York following a grand jury's failure to indict Wilson in the shooting death of Michael Brown that summer. Across the country, thousands marched—as they did during the Ferguson rebellion—and demanded justice for yet another Black child killed by state-sanctioned violence. In the New York City march, I saw women and men my age and younger. There were parents with their toddlers; families with

---

14. "Police Commissioner James P. O'Neill Announces Decision in Disciplinary Case of Officer Daniel Pantaleo," August 19, 2019, https://www1.nyc.gov.

grandparents. Parents and children carried signs, many of which displayed Garner's last words. Many of the individuals I talked with that night shared the same reason for marching: they, or someone they loved, could be the next name to end up on a board or hashtag. Others told me they were inspired to protest after seeing flyers that were shared on social media under the BLM hashtag. Some told me the march was an outlet for their anger and fears; one young woman that night cried out, "Why can't our kids be innocent and free from the trauma of violence and death?"

I heard similar sentiments in spring 2015, when I attended a protest following the death of twenty-five-year-old Freddie Gray, who was killed in Baltimore, Maryland. On April 12, Gray was arrested by police officers who alleged that he illegally possessed a knife. He was placed into a police van, where he suffered severe injuries during transportation. He fell into a coma and, six days later, died. On April 29, I joined my friend Enoch, who years later became my husband, and hundreds of marchers as we walked and chanted from Union Square to Forty-Second Street in Manhattan. Later that evening, as the march continued past Forty-Second Street, Enoch was arrested. I remember the way my heart stopped as I watched him being pulled into a police van. I feared for his life and wondered whether he, or any of the other individuals arrested that night, would be the next victim of police violence. I remember approaching a nearby police officer and asking where I could find my friend. She shrugged and answered, "Not my problem." I remember the urge to grab her, or any nearby officer. Activists held me back. They said it would not help me or my friend if I, too, got arrested. "It's going to be alright," many of them said, as they gave me the names of advocates and lawyers who regularly dealt with such arrests, many of which were mere NYPD scare tactics that happened often.

This was not my first interaction with the NYPD. Like many nonwhite citizens, our coming-of-age stories are always informed by our interactions with law enforcement: from the first time my sister, Pamela, and I were followed in pharmacies as children; to the night our father, the safest driver we know, was pulled over on our way home from a family dinner. The night of Enoch's arrest, I witnessed the power that American police officers possess, one which allows them to control, assault, and kill people of color in public spaces. I also knew that what I saw was nothing compared to the violence activists experienced the previous year during the Ferguson rebellion, a violence that many white Americans would experience for the first time during the antiracism protests of 2020 when footage of police brutality against white mothers and veterans who were standing in solidarity with Black Lives Matter erupted on social media. In June 2020 alone, persons involved in incidents with America's largest police department, the NYPD, included Jahmel Leach, a sixteen-year-old who was Tased and bruised in the Bronx by police officers;[15] Dounya Zayer, a twenty-year-old woman who was pushed by a police officer in Brooklyn and developed a concussion;[16] and Ricky Bellevue, a thirty-five-year-old man who was arrested and placed into a chokehold by a police officer in Queens.[17] As Americans across the country were calling for

15. Edgar Sandoval and Ashley Southall, "Injuries to Teenager during Protest Arrest Are under Investigation," *New York Times*, June 11, 2020, https://www.nytimes.com.

16. Ashley Southall, "Officer Who Violently Shoved Protester in Brooklyn Is Charged with Assault," *New York Times*, June 9, 2020, https://www.nytimes.com.

17. Ashley Southall and Mihir Zaveri, "After Video Shows Apparent Chokehold, N.Y.P.D. Suspends Officer," *New York Times*, June 21, 2020, https://www.nytimes.com.

the abolition of police departments, law enforcement continued to disregard the very values they falsely claimed to uphold
as an institution, choosing, instead, to continue in the violent
tradition that has existed since the first police department was
created in the nineteenth century, a history that I explore more
fully in later chapters. On the night of Enoch's arrest, something inside me shifted. While I would not critically engage
with abolition until 2020, I knew the NYPD, and all American
police departments like it, was not a collective body of women
and men committed to justice, safety, and the preservation of all
human life; they were committed to power.

I would not attend another protest until 2020, but I continued to carry that night with me. For years, I had nightmares
about my father's death. He was an interstate truck driver at the
time and drove throughout Maine, Ohio, Pennsylvania, North
Carolina, and Virginia, often into rural cities that had almost
no Black or immigrant populations. I feared that he would get
pulled over by law enforcement or chased down by an armed
white racist in a pickup truck. My father, Julio Cesar Segura,
is a warm, shy, and brilliant Black immigrant, who loves jazz
music and has an avid interest in extraterrestrials; he taught my
sister and me how to love music, poetry, and sports. These are
not the aspects of my father the U.S. Immigration and Customs
Enforcement saw when they stopped him along the Canadian
border in 2017, however; and it is not what countless racists
have seen since he arrived in the United States. White men
and women could look at people like him and see not a father
or husband but a Black body not worthy of living. For years
I remained consumed by negative feelings—always anxious,
weary, and angry. I learned that such feelings are not an anomaly. The footage of police violence, organizers and medical professionals have claimed for years, can cause anxiety, stress, and

even post-traumatic stress disorder, especially for African American women, men, and children. Monnica Williams, a clinical psychologist and the director of the Laboratory for Culture and Mental Health Disparities, states that police violence traumatizes Black communities. "There's a heightened sense of fear and anxiety when you feel like you can't trust the people who have been put in charge to keep you safe," she says, adding that along "with the everyday instances of racism, like microaggressions and discrimination," instances of police violence can lead "to a sense of alienation and isolation. It's race-based trauma."[18] Two days following the murder of Garner, ABC News aired a segment on his death that featured almost thirty seconds of his final seconds alive. Such proliferation of violence, Garza told me, demonstrates how Black women, men, and children, and all nonwhite citizens, have always been viewed as disposable in America. Every police shooting fuels the American fallacy that victims of police brutality are less innocent and therefore more deserving of violence, and why many people in America excuse police violence and murder. One of the goals of Black Lives Matter, Garza told me, is to fight for a world free of all of the systems that oppress and kill Black people—including policing and prisons. The movement, which quickly became the guiding tenet for organizers across the world, promotes an unrelenting commitment to human life and dignity. Garza, Tometi, and Cullors have created a decentralized community of activists who stand in solidarity with the rallying cry, "Black Lives Matter" and center the lived experiences of society's most vulnerable, Black transgender and queer women and men. They promote principles that shift power and resources away from privileged men and women and into the Black communities most harmed

---

18. Kenya Downs, "When black death goes viral, it can trigger PTSD-like trauma," PBS, July 22, 2016, https://www.pbs.org.

by systemic racism. Unlike the leaders of the church and traditions I seemed unable to shake, these women helped me to begin to reimagine my faith and identity as centered in the struggle toward Black liberation and the experiences of Black people in a church that often ignores our voices. "Black Lives Matter is not just about police violence," Garza told me. "It is about the ways in which Black people are denied a dignified life. That falls along the lines of gender and sexual assault and sexual harassment. That falls along the lines of nationality—not all Black people are born in the United States. That falls along the line of class."

Black Lives Matters also promotes a culture of discernment, or introspection. The founders encourage organizers who adopt the movement's mission to unlearn any internal biases and privileges one might carry as well. My BLM reporting has provided me the opportunity to refocus my energy outside my own experience and begin to acknowledge my own privilege as a Black immigrant with light skin, one not afforded to darker-skinned women, men, and children. Garza, Tometi, and Cullors taught me that in order to treat writing as a vocation, especially as a Catholic, I must begin to understand and reject racial capitalism, which is treated more fully later in the book, and work to reject the white supremacist indoctrination I have undergone since arriving in the United States. Black Lives Matter, Garza reminded me, is a movement that is guided, like my faith, by love, solidarity, and justice. These women have dedicated more than twenty years in their respective organizing careers toward the struggle for Black liberation. They are committed to ensuring that BLM helps to dismantle the systemic oppression caused by cisgender white women and men and to uplift the entirety of the Black experience, particularly people who are also marginalized within the Black community, such as transgender women and men who cannot pass. Their mission quickly became inextricable from my vocation as a writer: if our church leaders were not ready to dismantle our institution's white supremacy, then young Catholics, like me, must use the intersectional, anticapitalist, and Catholic framework of Black Lives Matter to demand a better church.

Black Lives Matter

Just weeks after I attended the marches demanding justice for Freddie Gray, Pope Francis published *Laudato si'* ("On Care for Our Common Home"). The encyclical, the second of his papacy, was written to help Catholics around the world understand the pope's position on climate change and the environment, and to subsequently guide our own thinking on these issues. "Men and women of our postmodern world run the risk of rampant individualism, and many problems of society are connected with today's self-centered culture of instant gratification," Francis writes. A focus on profit has created a culture that generates waste, destroys the planet, and burdens society's most vulnerable. He criticizes consumerism, calls on all people to work toward creating a more sustainable planet, and urges new approaches to combat homelessness and poverty. On reading *Laudato si'*, I immediately noticed similarities with the mission of the BLM movement. Both focused on social issues and called on us to reject the very individualism that was creating the problems we had to combat. Both challenged a world that was different from the oppressive one I knew. "The best way to restore men and women to their rightful place, putting an end to their claim to absolute dominion over the earth, is to speak once more of the figure of a Father who creates and who alone owns the world."[19]

---

19. Pope Francis, *Laudato si'*, no. 75, http://www.vatican.va.

However, the document, lauded and praised by many, makes no mention of the effects of climate change or capitalism on marginalized ethnic groups outside of its mentions of indigenous communities, including no reference to how women, men, and children of African descent have been exploited, tortured, and killed since the days of chattel slavery. There is no mention of the racial capitalism born out of slavery and its link to every form of oppression around the world, from American policing to the occupied territories in Palestine. In the United States alone, Black women make less money than white women, are more likely to be incarcerated, and face higher rates of sexual violence, especially Black transgender women. African Americans and Latinos, especially Puerto Rican Americans, are more likely to die from diseases such as asthma.[20] *Laudato si'*, unlike BLM, makes no mention of the ways gender intersects with issues like global warming. The only explicit mention of gender in the entire document is used to negate the very existence of transgender women, men, and children around the world:

> Learning to accept our body, to care for it and to respect its fullest meaning, is an essential element of any genuine human ecology. Also, valuing one's own body in its femininity or masculinity is necessary if I am going to be able to recognize myself in an encounter with someone who is different. In this way we can joyfully accept the specific gifts of another man or woman, the work of God the Creator, and find mutual enrichment. It is not a healthy attitude which would seek "to cancel out

---

20. See "Ethnic Disparities in the Burden and Treatment of Asthma," The Asthma and Allergy Foundation of America, https://www.aafa.org.

sexual difference because it no longer knows how to confront it." (no. 155)

Garza, Cullors, and Tometi, however, promote a movement that centers the lived experiences of those our church would rather ignore. This focus on the lived experiences of those in the LGBTQIA community owing to the queer and transgender people who risked their lives to protest in Ferguson in 2014. "We did little to ensure their visibility, to lift up the fact that our work is being advanced by an extraordinary number of Transwomen and men," writes Cullors. "The most criminalized people on the planet are Black Transwomen who cannot pass. We resolve, as a movement, to ensure that that never happens again."[21] Since Ferguson, she writes, the organization makes sure to always introduce, whenever talking about BLM, the organizing efforts of transgender and queer activists, and work with organizations that amplify Black transwomen, including the Marsha P. Johnson Institute and the Trans Women of Color Collective. Cullors is honest about her own privilege and how important it was for the founders to internalize and learn from these valid criticisms, critiques that helped to make the BLM's mission even stronger. They learned how to center and uplift a Black experience that was more marginalized than their own.

These Black female leaders, unlike the predominantly white, all-male bishops who oversee the U.S. Catholic Church, are genuine examples of Christian leadership. Like Christ, the founders fight for the marginalized, advocate for peace and justice, and work to dismantle oppressive systems. The movement's religious undertones have a lot to do with the respective religious

---

21. Patrisse Khan-Cullors and Asha Bandele, *When They Call You a Terrorist: A Black Lives Matter Memoir* (New York: St. Martin's Press, 2018), 216.

upbringings of Tometi and Cullors, who both grew up in religious homes. While Cullors has moved away from her faith and identifies as spiritually always seeking, Tometi currently identifies as a Christian. Her faith and work are influenced by liberation theology, a movement in Christianity. According to Gustavo Gutiérrez Merino, a Peruvian theologian and priest who is considered one of its founders, liberation theology calls on Catholics to study Jesus's teachings through the experiences of the world's most marginalized people, using the economic theories of Friedrich Engels and Karl Marx. Like liberation theology, Black Lives Matter prioritizes the experiences of the poorest and most oppressed. Garza told me that what began as an online campaign in 2013 quickly grew into a global network with chapters all over the country. The movement promotes solidarity and communal power and rejects individualism through a decentralized structure. It seeks to dismantle the systems that have oppressed *all* Americans and to give people the language to analyze critically how the United States became one of the most powerful countries in the world. Since its birth on the back of chattel slavery, this country has given white Americans, with the help of law enforcement, privileges and advantages that have allowed them to continue to oppress and kill nonwhite Americans. This is why, the movement proclaims, no one is liberated unless all Black people are free.

Despite this messaging, for years since its birth, critics and the media, particularly after Ferguson, whose impact I describe more fully in the next chapter, have depicted Black Lives Matter as disorganized, exclusive, and violent. Civil rights activist Barbara Reynolds wrote in the *Washington Post* that she supported the mission's "cause, but not its approach";[22] and a writer in *The Guardian* described the movement as "so ubiquitous as to have

---

22. Barbara Reynolds, "I Was a Civil Rights Activist in the 1960s.

lost almost all meaning" and merely an outlet "for people to endlessly repeat 'I hate racism' while doing nothing to actually stop it."[23] Within the Catholic Church, I encountered Catholics who shared similar opinions about the movement. Many described it as violent toward law enforcement, racist toward white Americans, similar to the Ku Klux Klan, and committed to pushing a pro-abortion agenda. Additionally, many Catholics are critical of the movement's rejection of capitalism—despite the anticapitalist lens Francis has encouraged us to develop throughout his entire papacy—with many telling me that a movement that criticizes the only "successful" economic system could not really be concerned with improving Black life in the United States.[24] Both secular and Christian critics demonstrated how quickly white Americans disregard a movement that centers Black, queer women. I asked Garza what she believed were the movement's biggest successes. She told me that Black Lives Matter has assisted in the passing of criminal justice reform, pointing to President Barack Obama's commuting of sentences

But It's Hard for Me to Get behind Black Lives Matter," August 24, 2015, https://www.washingtonpost.com.

23. Joseph Harker, "'Black Lives Matter' Risks Becoming an Empty Slogan. It's Not Enough to Defeat Racism," June 11, 2020, https://www.theguardian.com.

24. For example, Black Lives Matter presents a more nuanced and intersectional understanding of reproductive justice than the Catholic Church. In 2016, Garza described reproductive justice as "very much situated within the Black Lives Matter movement," adding that reproductive justice was "not just about the right for women to be able to determine when and how and where they want to start families, but it is also very much about our right to be able to raise families, to be able to raise children to become adults." The latter, she added, is consistently hindered by state-sanctioned violence. See https://www.colorlines.com/articles/black-lives-matter-partners-reproductive-justice-groups-fight-black-women.

for more than 7,000 people while he was in office. In 2015, he commuted the sentences of 46 offenders with drug charges, and two years later, he commuted the sentences of 330 inmates serving time at the federal level for drug charges. Throughout his four years in office, Obama granted more than 1,000 commutations, the most granted by any American president.[25] The organization's work has also led to the removal of corrupt politicians and "a new international dialogue about the pervasiveness and endurance of racism." Since 2013, Garza, Tometi, and Cullors have also inspired countless young Black and Brown women and men, like myself, to use our vocation in the struggle for Black liberation. This movement has been my generation's—and the Catholic Church's—call to action.

The Fight for a Liberated Church

No American institution, including the Catholic Church, is free of internalized white supremacy, yet very few white Catholic bishops or faith leaders are willing to name and condemn publicly the ways that racist ideals have been internalized by the United States Conference of Catholic Bishops (USCCB). The Black Lives Matter movement taught me how to analyze and critique the USCCB's racial justice efforts, from its 1979 letter on racism to its unwillingness to opine on issues like police brutality and abolition. By internalizing the movement's mission, I understood that, as Catholics and as a church committed to the resurrection of Christ, we were to fight for the dismantling of the white supremacy that has existed within our church for

---

25. "President Obama Has Now Granted More Commutations than Any President in this Nation's History," The White House. President Barack Obama Blog, January 17, 2017, https://obamawhite house.archives.gov.

hundreds of years. M. Shawn Copeland, an emerita professor at Boston College, is known for her intersectional theological work, which covers politics, anthropology, and Black Catholic theology. In *Knowing Christ Crucified: The Witness of African-American Religious Experience,* she writes that "theology must work out the relation between the murderous crucifixion of Jesus of Nazareth and the murderous crucifixion of countless poor, excluded, and despised children, women, and men," adding, "we who are followers of the crucified Jesus must protest the oppression and suffering of each human person and work for their flourishing." For the future of the church in the United States, our white faith leaders must join the struggle for Black liberation. This begins by acknowledging and engaging with the BLM movement and its founders.

Black Lives Matter is not a movement pushing an extremist agenda that contradicts our faith; it is the secular version of our Catholic social teaching. It is a decentralized movement that promotes Black life and dignity, emphasizes the need for community and empathy, centers the most marginalized and vulnerable in society, and rejects capitalism. Along with helping millennials and others of the digital age unlearn American history, the movement has inspired a generation of younger activists and given them the tools and language to learn how to organize. Following a racist incident at the University of Missouri that involved a racial slur against Black students and mishandling by the school's administration, activists protested for almost a month until the school's president, Tim Wolfe, resigned. The movement pushed antiracism efforts to the forefront of a generation that was coming of age amid the very digital tools the movement used to spread its messages. It brought the treatment that African Americans across the country have faced for centuries to the forefront of the white American consciousness.

It is becoming clear that the first step leaders must take is the very message the USCCB actively and consistently proclaims: as Catholics, we are called to encounter and learn from all experiences, including those most unlike our own. As a body of mostly white, all male Catholics, the USCCB can begin to reject the systemic oppression present in the American church by meeting with the founders and organizers of the Black Lives Matter movement. In 2018, I asked Garza if the Black Lives Matter movement would welcome the presence of Catholic clergy. The question and Garza's answer now seem more prescient than ever: "There's such a gap between the practice of our values and the statement of our values. Unless that gets addressed, it's hard for me to imagine that the church, that the Catholic Church in particular, would close that gap."

After years of reporting on the movement, I finally see white leaders and corporations, including Twitter, Netflix, A24, and the NFL, publicly declaring support for the Black Lives Matter movement. Since 2013, public opinion of the movement has also changed. Data published by the *New York Times* on June 10, 2020, showed that American support for the movement grew by a twenty-eight-point margin over two weeks, or "by nearly as much as it had over the previous two years." We also saw a shift in the rhetoric used by white men—and women—in and outside the Catholic Church. On June 1, 2020, Bishop Mark J. Seitz kneeled and held a Black Lives Matter poster during an eight-minute prayer for George Floyd in El Paso, Texas. When asked why he knelt in solidarity with the fight for Black liberation, Seitz declared, "To say, as all who eat from the table of the Eucharist should be able to say, that Black lives matter is just another way of repeating something we in the United States seem to so often forget, that God has a special love for the forgotten and oppressed."[26]

---

26. Rhina Guidos, "After 'taking a knee,' border bishop gets call

Faith leaders in California, including Bishop Robert McElroy, called for law enforcement reform and for an end to police violence.[27] Bishop Robert McElroy stated:

> Ours must not be an episodic response that seeks to calm the waters of racial turmoil and then return to normalcy. The only authentic moral response to this moment in our nation's history is a sustained conversion of heart and soul to genuinely comprehend the overwhelming evil of racism in our society, and to refuse to rest until we have rooted it out.[28]

Public declarations are a welcome—albeit long overdue—first step from individual church bishops. However, this is not nearly enough to build a liberated and resurrected church. In almost ten years of reporting on race and Catholicism, I have seen our bishops fail repeatedly in their racial justice efforts, from their 2018 pastoral letter on racism to their refusal to collectively declare that "Black Lives Matter" in 2020. White men in the church, from our priests to our bishops, have historically benefitted from white supremacy. When these same men use their power, privilege, and platforms to proclaim that Black Lives Matter, other white people with similar access will listen. If our bishops declare that Black liberation is inextricable from our faith, then white Catholics and, more broadly, Americans will hopefully feel inspired to stand in solidarity with the fight for Black

---

from pope, releases statement," *Angelus News*, June 4, 2020, https://angelusnews.com.

27. CBS News 8 Team, Alicia Summers, "San Diego Faith Leaders Call for Law Enforcement Reform, End of Police Brutality," CBS8, June 11, 2020, https://www.cbs8.com.

28. Bishop Robert McElroy, "Finding Grace Within Our Republic of Suffering," June 1, 2020, https://www.sdcatholic.org.

life. "No one has greater love than this, to lay down one's life for one's friends" (John 15:13). To be in solidarity, to truly show that the U.S. Church cares about Black lives, our bishops must enter into dialogue with Garza, Cullors, and Tometi. Along with the sudden declarations in support of the movement, individuals and organizations in the church must also internalize the beliefs attached to this label, including its emphasis on creating a world where men are not centered. This means giving nonwhite women the space to lead and mentor, from boardrooms to magazines. This means encouraging Catholic parishes, schools, and media to create spaces for these communities at their respective tables, especially for African Americans, who, for over four hundred years, have been the creators of the most cherished aspects of U.S. culture, including music, fashion, and sports. Our society appropriates Black culture while simultaneously devaluing Black life: African American women have higher numbers of maternal death rates than any other group in the country; and Black men make up almost 40 percent of the prison population. Economic racial disparities are the highest they have ever been. For example, a 2019 study revealed the huge gap between the median wealth held by Black families ($17,000) and white families ($171,000)—a ratio of ten to one.[29] The time is now for white Americans to sacrifice their power and allow Black people to create and lead our new and more equitable world.

For all white Catholics, start by learning from me and the women who shaped me, including the Black women who have taught a generation of young Catholics how to think, learn, and fight for the most marginalized people in our communities. These women are the blueprint to becoming a church that replaces white supremacy and privilege with white sacrifice.

---

29. Congressman Don Beyer, "The Economic State of America in 2020," Joint Economic Committee, https://www.jec.senate.gov.

2

The Black Women of the Movement

I always knew I wanted to be a writer. I began learning English months after my arrival in the United States and would, for a few years, struggle to perfect it. Every night, I read along as a cassette tape recited a book; the exercise, repetitive in nature, made certain words and phrases familiar to my young brain. My translating work started soon after I became fluent. It was, at times, humiliating, and, at other times, a power I held over my mother in stores, doctors' offices, and supermarkets, where I translated her Spanish words to English-speaking citizens around us. *"¡Esto es demasiado caro! Pregúntale si puede bajar el precio"* ("This is too expensive! Ask him to lower the price"), or, *"Como que dijo que no? Pregúntale una vez más y dile que no me voy"* ("What do you mean he said 'no'? Ask him again and tell him I will not leave").

Years later, in my late twenties, as I rummaged through relics of my parents' first year in the United States, I found a letter my mother wrote to me while I was still in Santo Domingo, one she never showed me until I was an adult. In the letter, dated December 8, 1990, my parents' first day in America, she described the fear of boarding a plane to a new country, the feeling of winter winds on their island skin, the pain of leaving their daughter behind. *"Yo le pedi casi entre sueno a Dios que nos ayudara a salir adelante y que nos cuidara nuestra hija, que nuestra separacion es par el bien de ella y que pronto estaremos juntos de nuevo—con la ayuda de Dios.*" Her writing, like her speech, is beautiful, melodic, and prayerful. In this letter, like many others, she asked God to pray over her and my father and her firstborn back on the island. Their sacrifice, she wrote, was to give me, and every other relative who followed in their footsteps to America, a better life. Soon, she concluded, we would be together again. Her hope, then and now, is rooted in her Catholic faith—an unwavering love and trust in her relationship with God. She prays daily and fervently, like in this letter, for a better world, for those she loves. She showed my sister and me how to love and respect others, how to be patient, and how to work hard. My mother taught me how to be a woman of faith, how to speak for myself and others, and how to be a Catholic storyteller. With these skills and faith, in 2014, two years into my first job in media, I began to report on the Black Lives Matter movement.

Policing in the United States

The Black Lives Matter movement was formed in 2013 to highlight the ways anti-Black violence is engrained in every American institution. "It's been happening for so long that we even have a language to talk about why it's okay for vigilantes and police to kill Black people with no due process," Garza told me. "The language that we use is, 'Well, if they hadn't been committing a crime, then there would not have been a problem.'" The movement sheds light on the violence, particularly at the hands of law enforcement, that has always been directed against Black and indigenous Americans since the latter fought against the first European colonizers. Like Black liberation movements before it, BLM is critical of the ways that racial capitalism exploits and oppresses Black Americans, from young TikTok influencers, whose work is constantly plagiarized by white people, to unpaid student athletes, whose colleges make millions off their names and faces, to the Kardashian family, many of whom have gotten famous by appropriating Black culture.[1] In July, 2016, Alton Sterling and Philando Castile, two Black men, were shot within a span of twenty-four hours by Baton Rouge, Louisiana, and St. Anthony, Minnesota, police department officers, respectively.[2] Garza called for the defunding of police departments. She reminded Americans that the struggle toward liberation must include drastically shifting the power given to American law enforcement.[3] Police departments are descendants of U.S. chattel slavery. The movement challenges Americans in the digital age to think about how the United States has used its policing to destroy and destabilize diasporic communities in America and around the world.

In 1838, the Boston police department became the first modern policing institution in the United States.[4] Prior to Boston, however, white Americans created unofficial "slave patrols," which served as local law enforcement groups that operated differently from state to state. This meant that in Southern states, for example, the groups were used for controlling Black

---

1. Lindsay Peoples, "An Open Letter to My White Friends Who Love the Kardashians," *The Cut*, July 20, 2015, https://www.thecut.com.

2. Leah Donnella, "Two Days, Two Deaths: The Police Shootings of Alton Sterling and Philando Castile," NPR Code Switch, July 7, 2016, https://www.npr.org.

3. Racahell Davis, "Black Lives Matter Co-Founder Alicia Garza Talks Philando Castile, Alton Sterling and How You Can Get Involved in Fighting Injustice," *Essence*, July 8, 2016, https://www.essence.com.

4. "The History of Police in Creating Social Order in the U.S.," NPR.org, June 5, 2020, www.npr.org.

Americans who tried to escape enslavement; and in the North, the predecessors to the police focused on repressing any kind of rebellion or strike by laborers. American policing was created out of a need to control violently those who went against the status quo. By 1857, additional departments were created in New York City, New Orleans, Cincinnati, Newark, Baltimore, and Philadelphia. By the twentieth century, the country saw major changes to policing, thanks to August Vollmer, the first police chief of the Berkeley, California, police department, established in 1909. As chief, Vollmer introduced new policing policies to his department, including lie detector tests, a police records system, police training schools, and mounted officers. He also helped to militarize U.S. police departments. Years after he served in the military, Vollmer credited his time fighting in the Spanish-American War with teaching him the "military tactics" needed because at the end of the day, Vollmer espoused, police officers were "conducting a war, a war against the enemies of society and we must never forget that." His training schools, which were implemented nationally, were centered on "the coercive institutions and practices of the imperial state that create and sustain empire," which refer to "colonial conquest, the violent suppression of anticolonial dissent, and counterinsurgency operations." Police adopted many of these reforms across the country.

At the University of California, Vollmer was the head of their criminal justice program, where his "students took courses in which they learned about different 'racial types' and how 'hereditary' and 'race degeneration' led to criminality."[5] These sentiments were internalized by U.S. police departments

---

5. Julian Go, "The Imperial Origins of American Policing: Militarization and Imperial Feedback in the Early 20th Century," *American Journal of Sociology* 125, no. 5 (2020): 1214.

across the country, many of which have also been infiltrated by white supremacist groups such as the Ku Klux Klan.[6] Between 2018 and 2019 alone, police officers shot and killed at least two thousand Americans. Black Americans are viewed by law enforcement as more suspicious than white Americans, a sentiment that emboldens nonlaw enforcement persons, like George Zimmerman, to treat Black citizens as dangerous and therefore disposable. Two-thirds of 8,000 police officers surveyed across the country view police shootings as "isolated incidents" that have nothing to do with larger social issues. Black and Brown communities are less likely to rate police officers highly.[7] In 2020 alone, the list of Black women and men killed by police includes Tina Marie Davis, a fifty-three-year-old mother killed by police in Spring Valley, New York; Breonna Taylor, a twenty-six-year-old emergency medical technician shot and killed by police while she slept in her Louisville, Kentucky, home; Tony McDade, a thirty-eight-year-old Black transgender man shot and killed by police in Tallahassee, Florida; Mubarak Soulemane, nineteen, shot and killed by police in West Haven, Connecticut; Lebarron Ballard, twenty-eight, shot and killed by police in Abilene, Texas; Kanisha Necole Fuller, forty-three, shot and killed in Birmingham, Alabama; Modesto Reyes, thirty-five, shot and killed by police in Marrero, Louisiana; Malik Canty, thirty-five, shot and killed by officers in Paterson, New Jersey; and Dijon Kizzee, twenty-nine, shot and killed by police in Los Angeles, California.

Another form of police brutality is sexual assault. Chattel

---

6. Alice Speri, "The FBI Has Quietly Investigated White Supremacist Infiltration of Law Enforcement," The Intercept, January 13, 2017, https://theintercept.com.

7. Dalia Fahmy, et al, "10 things we know about race and policing in the U.S.," Pew Research Center, https://www.pewresearch.org.

slavery created an economic system in which white men tortured and raped enslaved Black women and children, who were then subsequently forced to give birth to the resulting children. Policing was born out of the same anti-Black violence that allowed Americans to justify—and which continues to excuse—the violence of enslavement, from slavery to prison. Police departments across the United States are equipped with resources that allow them to physically assault and restrain citizens at any given moment. Along with guns, tasers, handcuffs, and rubber bullets, law enforcement also uses sexual violence as a tool. This includes cavity searches and rape; the latter is one of the most common complaints filed against police officers. David Correia writes:

> Under chattel slavery, Black people were deemed legal property (see no humans involved), and Black women and children were subjected to rape, forced pregnancies, and other forms of sexual violence. The police rape of Black and Brown women today not only belongs to this history, but is directly structured by it, as their bodies are essentially rendered property of the state when in police custody. Similarly, rape has been a central settler colonial weapon of disciplining and dominating Indigenous women and children, and it isn't a surprise that cops have been implicated in the murders and disappearances of Indigenous women, as the Murdered and Missing Indigenous Women (MMIW) movement in Canada has helped to make visible (see also starlight tour).[8]

---

8. David Correia, *Police: A Field Guide* (Brooklyn, NY: Verso, 2018), 98.

Garza helped me to contextualize this history. I traced a line from chattel slavery to Jim Crow to the first police departments in the United States and to the many Black women who have been assaulted and killed by law enforcement, including twenty-eight-year-old Atatiana Jefferson, who was shot and killed by an officer in Fort Worth, Texas in 2019; thirty-year-old Charleena Lyles, who was pregnant and shot by police in Seattle, Washington in 2017; sixty-six-year-old Deborah Danner, who was shot and killed by the NYPD in her home in the Bronx in 2016; and twenty-eight-year-old Sandra Bland, who died in police custody in Waller County, Texas in 2015. "Policing as a system is incredibly corrupt, period. There are people inside of these departments who want to reinstate a level of integrity into these departments and they should be commended. But they cannot do that on their own," Garza told me, adding, "Policing as a whole in this country is deeply, deeply corrupt and cannot be reformed."

Cullors, Tometi, and Garza

After my interview with Garza, I read *When They Call You a Terrorist: A Black Lives Matter Memoir*, co-authored by Patrisse Cullors and Asha Bandele in 2018. Cullors's words provide a poignant reflection of her life. She was born in 1983 in Los Angeles, California. Growing up, her family lived in the Pacoima neighborhood of the city, where Cullors, her brothers, and community—a majority of whom were Latino—were constantly harassed by the Los Angeles police department. At the age of twelve, Cullors was arrested for the first time. "The cop tells me to come to the front of the room, where he handcuffs me in front of everyone and takes me to the dean's office, where my bag is searched, where I am searched, pockets turned out, shoes checked, just like my brothers in the alleyway when

I was nine years old." At a young age, she joined the Bus Riders Union, an LA-based civil rights group; and when she was just sixteen years old, she was forced to leave her family home after telling them that she was queer. These experiences inform Cullors's entire advocacy, from working as the executive director of the Coalition to End Sheriff Violence in Los Angeles Jails to the BLM movement she founded with Tometi and Garza, the latter of whom she met in 2005 in Rhode Island. Cullors's work felt revolutionary. In my socio-political awakening, her autobiography revealed that the parts of my life that I was desperately trying to hide—my diasporic roots and growing up in one of the most impoverished counties in the United States—all informed my journalism and faith.

After the hashtag #BlackLivesMatter was added to Garza's 2013 Facebook post, the two connected with Tometi, whom Garza met in 2012. Tometi was born in Phoenix, Arizona, in 1984, to Nigerian immigrants. Tometi, who was influenced by liberation theology, has always considered faith to be an integral part of her life. Her family is Christian, and her parents started a church to help African immigrants new to the United States. For over fifteen years, she has been committed to fighting for human rights. She has served as the editorial director of the first U.S. immigrant rights organization for Africans, the Black Alliance for Just Immigration. Her professional career paid particular attention to the issues facing the African immigrant population. In the United States, almost 5 percent of the country's immigration population consists of African immigrants; there are just over two million African immigrants, the majority of whom are from Nigeria, Ghana, Ethiopia, Somalia, and South Africa. During a BBC interview in 2019, Tometi commented:

> Black Lives Matter originally started as a rallying cry. It sent chills throughout our entire community, made

all of us feel a great sense of pain, but also outrage. And for myself, I had two younger brothers. It was going to mark them for the rest of time and it was going to be such an important historical moment in all of our lives. . . . I believe there is more visibility about anti-black racism and just structural racism, period, in the United States. And I believe the movement that is way bigger than myself and the two co-founders of Black Lives Matter has ushered in a type of conversation and politic that says: "You're not going to turn away from these issues of injustice that are happening and playing this society."[9]

These women gave people the template to talk both eloquently and accessibly about our politics, our social justice concerns, and our identities. I began to see myself "as part of the global Black family," yet with the understanding that as an Afro-Dominican immigrant, I was "aware of the different ways we are impacted or privileged as Black people who exist in different parts of the world." I began to research and follow online thinkers, such as cultural critic Zahira Kelly, who inspired in me what it means to be a part of the diaspora, what it means to be "peoples of African origin living outside of the continent." Everything I read, I wrote about, privately, most of it unpublished; reading and writing empowered me to reject "the light grip of heteronormative thinking, or rather, the belief that all in the world are heterosexual (unless s/he or they disclose otherwise)." BLM used language that galvanized writers, poets, artists, and teachers into action. Cullors, Tometi, and Garza also demonstrated the power of self-accountability.

---

9. Daniel Henry, "African Diaspora Diaries: Opal Tometi," BBC World News 3-part series, February 23, 2019, https://www.bbc.co.uk.

Black, Equitable, and Just

In *When They Call You a Terrorist*, Cullors writes about a criticism the movement received in 2014 following BLM's first in-person gathering with the Black Lives Matter Freedom Ride to Ferguson. On August 9, 2014, eighteen-year-old Michael Brown Jr. was shot and killed by police officer Darren Wilson. On the day of Brown's death, Wilson alleged that Brown fled after an altercation. The officer then proceeded to chase the Black teenager and subsequently shoot him six times. He alleged that Brown attacked him, a claim denied by twenty-two-year-old Dorian Johnson, Brown's friend, who was present when he died. After his death, Brown's body was left in the streets by the city's law enforcement for more than four hours. Keeanga-Yamahtta Taylor, a historian, professor, and columnist at the *New Yorker*, describes the city after Brown's lynching:

> After Brown's body was finally moved, residents erected a makeshift memorial of teddy bears and memorabilia on the spot where police had left his body. When the police arrived with a canine unit, one officer let a dog urinate on the memorial. Later, when Brown's mother, Lesley McSpadden, laid out rose petals in the form of his initials, a police cruiser whizzed by, crushing the memorial and scattering the flowers. The next evening, McSpadden and other friends and family went back to the memorial site and laid down a dozen roses. Again, a police cruiser came through and destroyed the flowers. Later that night, the uprising began.[10]

---

10. Keeanga-Yamahtta Taylor, *From #BlackLivesMatter to Black Liberation* (Chicago: Haymarket Books, 2016), 154.

From my home in the Bronx, I followed the moments of this uprising, all prolifically shared on Twitter and Instagram. I followed activists such as Johnetta Elzie, born and raised in St. Louis, who arrived in Ferguson and began tweeting the day of Brown's death. On August 9, Elzie posted, "It's still blood on the ground where Mike Brown Jr. was murdered. A cone in place where his body laid for hours today." For countless people outside Ferguson, Twitter conveyed the violence the protestors were facing daily from law enforcement. Mainstream media outlets, institutions with their own racially oppressive histories, seemed almost complicit in the campaign smear against the movement. Activists and journalists on the front lines, however, used Twitter to highlight the harassment and violence often incited by police officers; and often, as viewers from all over the world tuned in to refresh timelines in real time, conversations around pertinent issues surfaced on Twitter. For many, Ferguson introduced them to the Black Lives Matter movement.

Cullors writes that queer and transgender people were some of the most visible faces on the ground during the Ferguson uprising that summer. Despite this, she notes, coverage of the movement focused almost exclusively on cisgender Black women and men. In recent years, over a hundred transgender women and men have been killed in the United States, including, in 2020 alone, Dustin Parker, a twenty-five-year-old trans man killed in McAlester, Oklahoma; Monika Diamond, a thirty-five-year-old trans woman killed in Charlotte, North Carolina; and Helle Jae O'Regan, a twenty-year-old trans woman shot and killed in San Antonio, Texas. A disproportionate number of these deaths were Black transgender women; out of the twenty-two deaths in 2019 alone, almost all were Black women.[11] In spite of the violence trans women and men face daily, many trav-

---

11. Sarah McBride, "HRC Releases Annual Report on Epidemic

eled through unsafe cities on their way to Ferguson. The Black Lives Matter movement founders used this critique as a learning experience, and after Ferguson, the founders acknowledged their mistake and committed to uplifting those in the queer and transgender community. The Black Lives Matter movement, they declared, would always affirm and support trans women, men, and children and center their lived experience.

Cullors helped me to understand how Black women, throughout American history, have served as the true, often forgotten heroes of virtually every racial justice effort in the United States. "It is [Black] women," Cullors writes, "who are out there, often with their children, calling for an end to police violence, saying, 'We have a right to raise our children without fear.' But it's not women's courage that is showcased in the media."[12] This is because Black womanhood is threatened every day in the United States. Black girls are twice as likely to be suspended from school as white girls, and compared to white women, Black women face higher risks of domestic violence, are more likely to be murdered by their partners, and are more likely to be imprisoned.[13] BLM's focus on the experiences of Black women is significant because it taught a generation of young organizers how to create inclusive language in affirming spaces and policies focused on reparations for the years of oppression Black women and men have faced. BLM founders and organizers drafted policy, making concrete efforts to be more inclusive and affirming, and helped to launch

of Anti-Transgender Violence," Human Rights Campaign, November 18, 2019, https://www.hrc.org.

12. Khan-Cullors and Bandele, *When They Call You a Terrorist*, 219.

13. Asha DuMonthier, Chandra Childers, Ph.D., and Jessica Milli, Ph.D., "The Status of Black Women in the United States." Retrieved September 29, 2020, https://www.domesticworkers.org/sites/default/files/SOBW_report2017_compressed.pdf.

a movement focused on demanding justice for the female victims of police brutality.

Since its birth in 2013, the Black Lives Matter movement has given Americans a template for the world they envisioned—one that was Black, equitable, and just.

The Church's Reckoning

In 2019, I wrote that the church should emulate Nikole Hannah-Jones's 1619 Project, which sought to trace the effects of slavery throughout the history of the United States, a topic that is discussed in the next chapter. Creating a similar timeline but focused on Catholic U.S. history, I wrote that our church leaders could begin to show the Black community that they were genuinely committed to holding themselves accountable and fighting for liberation. Instead of waiting for the secular media to expose Catholic ties to slavery—like the *New York Times* did with the Society of Jesus in 2016—the timeline would allow our bishops to be transparent about the Catholic Church's connections to slavery, from the identity of the bishops who owned enslaved persons to the teachings of the church on racism.

How can we have a church in which reparations and public atonements are actively and consistently made for the sins of clerical sexual abuse but not for the sins of slavery, the very system that sixteenth-century Catholic leaders created? More than twelve million Africans were violently kidnapped and chained in ships. Millions died, as Black women, men, and children were forced to travel over the Atlantic Ocean to countries such as the United States, Brazil, and the Dominican Republic. From the early 1500s to the end of slavery in 1865, when the last enslaved Americans were freed in Texas, the United States received almost half a million enslaved Africans, who built everything from plantations and railroads to Wall Street. Enslaved women and men were separated from their partners, their children; and Black women were raped and impregnated by slave owners. This is the history of how our country was born, how the American Catholic Church was born. If the church wants to show it is ready to join the fight for Black liberation, then it must hold itself accountable. This begins by aligning itself with the women who created the Black Lives Matter movement.

While the U.S. Conference of Catholic Bishops continues to remain unwilling to reckon with its white supremacist roots, Cullors, Garza, and Tometi are teaching Catholics, and all Americans, what it truly means to fight for the most marginalized groups in our society, what it means to truly care about human life, and what it means to truly imagine a better and more Christ-like world. Unlike the church I love, these women are not afraid to demand a world "free from sexism, misogyny, and environments in which men are centered."[14]

In *When They Call You a Terrorist*, Cullors describes the complicated relationship she had with her mother's faith as a Jehovah's Witness. As a Black, queer woman, she writes that her mother's Christianity did "not feel liberating or purposeful—beyond the purpose of shaming and scaring us," adding that she wanted "a place of worship that feels honest," gave "mentorship and guidance," and that would help her become her "truest self."[15]

What does such a church, one that is authentic and committed to helping marginalized voices truly look like? One that uses not just its teaching but its land and money to fight for Black

---

14. Black Lives Matter, "What We Believe," https://blacklives matter.com/what-we-believe (2020).

15. Khan-Cullors and Bandele, *When They Call You a Terrorist*, 71.

liberation? American bishops can move us toward this church by incorporating the work of Cullors, Garza, and Tometi in a pastoral letter dedicated solely to the movement and by inviting the women to speak at church-sponsored panels with church bishops. By incorporating the work of Black, queer women, our church leaders can demonstrate that they want to create a church that vehemently condemns racism and white supremacy, centers and uplifts Black Americans, and truly believes that we "are the image of the Mother Church."

In a world that oppresses Black people, our church fathers can create a space that centers, learns from, and financially supports the scholars, thinkers, professors, and writers doing antiracism research that the church can more broadly integrate into ministry. This includes providing antiracism resources and training for those who are preparing to receive the sacraments. Another church is possible if we let Black women lead.

3

Chattel Slavery and
the Catholic Church

After belonging to this church for almost thirty years, I learned,
in 2020—thanks to the work of Shannen Dee Williams—that
chattel slavery in the United States began with the Catholic
Church. She writes that the Catholic Church was responsible
for the introduction of slavery into the United States, beginning
in the South in the 1500s:

> After slavery, most white Catholic religious orders of
> men and women and seminaries continued systemati-
> cally excluding African-descended people, especially
> U.S.-born black people, from admission on the basis of
> race well into the 20th century.
>
> The archival, oral history and written record is also
> littered with heart-wrenching examples of white Catho-
> lics subjecting black and brown Catholics to humili-
> ating segregation and exclusion in white-led parishes,
> schools, hospitals, convents, seminaries and neighbor-
> hoods.[1]

---

1. Williams, "If Racial Justice and Peace," http://thedialog.org.

Colonizers who had arrived in the colonies that became the United States, like those in the Caribbean, originally enslaved Native Americans, but as they died off—due to new diseases and violence from Europeans—they were replaced with enslaved Africans. During the transatlantic slave trade, Black people, whom colonizers viewed as mere property, were kidnapped, tortured, and sold from their homes in Senegal, Congo, Angola, and Ghana. For hundreds of years, slave traders from Portugal, England, France, the Netherlands, and Spain used the slave trade to transport more than millions of enslaved persons to the Americas; and in the summer of 1619, enslaved persons were forcibly taken to Jamestown, Virginia. Almost half a million Africans were enslaved and sold in the United States. Nikole Hannah-Jones, a staff writer at the *New York Times* who conceived of and spearheaded The 1619 Project, wrote that enslaved persons built the cotton economy that would keep many white American families rich for generations. Black people "grew and picked the cotton that at the height of slavery was the nation's most valuable commodity, accounting for half of all American exports and 66 percent of the world's supply." Enslaved people built our nation's railroads, the White House, the plantations of presidents George Washington and Thomas Jefferson. Hannah-Jones wrote that Wall Street was built by "the relentless buying, selling, insuring and financing of [Black] bodies and the products of their labor."[2] According to historian Tiya Miles, in New York, slaveholders, who consisted of 40 percent of all New York households, lent money to plantation owners in the South. "The value of bought bodies" was covered with insurance "policies from New York insurance companies."[3] By 1787, the U.S.

---

2. Nikole Hannah-Jones, "The Idea of America," in *The 1619 Project* (New York: New York Times Magazine, 2019), 16.

3. Tiya Miles, "Chained Migration," in *The 1619 Project*, 22.

Constitution was drafted. This document, still romanticized as the backbone of alleged American democracy more than two hundred years later and written by free white men, made no mention of slavery. This would change a year later with the "Three-Fifths Compromise," which stated:

> Representatives and direct Taxes shall be apportioned among the several States which may be included within this Union, according to their respective Numbers, which shall be determined by adding to the whole Number of free Persons, including those bound to Service for a Term of Years, and excluding Indians not taxed, three fifths of all other Persons.[4]

Until the Thirteenth Amendment, which abolished slavery in 1865, Black people were not considered free, full human beings. And even though they helped to create the democracy that white supremacists cling to in the twenty-first century, Black people would continue to be disenfranchised in the post-abolition period.

During the Reconstruction Era (1865 to 1877), Black Americans helped to create some of the biggest advances following the Civil War, including antidiscrimination laws, public schools, and the passage of the Fifteenth Amendment, which gave African American men the right to vote. By the 1900s, however, new laws, including poll taxes and literacy tests, would prevent Black men from voting. In 1913, Woodrow Wilson, the twenty-eighth U.S. president, legalized segregation. By the 1930s, cities known as Sundown Towns were preventing Black women, men,

---

4. U.S. House of Representatives, "Proportional Representation," U.S. Constitution, article I, section 2, clause 3, https://history.house.gov.

and children from entering into their communities after dark. Many of these communities were filled with members of the Ku Klux Klan, a U.S. terrorist organization, which grew to over one million members during this decade and was responsible for "hangings, floggings, mutilations, tarring and featherings, kidnappings, brandings by acid, along with a new intimidation tactic, cross-burnings."[5]

The 1619 Project

Technological advances in the twentieth century led to newer methods of violence against Black Americans. White doctors and scientists, still glorified in their respective fields today, would torture Black people in the name of medicine and reinforce myths, such as Black Americans felt less pain than whites and "had weak lungs that could be strengthened through hard work." These lies, wrote Linda Villarosa in The 1619 Project, made their way into medicine, thanks to men such as the physician J. Marion Sims, who, before the invention of anesthesia, performed operations on Black women, and physician and professor Samuel Cartwright, who claimed that "enslaved people were prone to a 'disease of the mind' called drapetomania, which caused them to run away from their enslavers." The internalizing of such lies into the American health-care system has created very real and dangerous disparities felt in 2020, including inadequate pain management and disproportionate maternal mortality rates for Black women. Villarosa also described a study that found that white medical students were more likely to believe that Black people "have thicker skin than do white

5. "The FBI Versus the Klan, Part 2: Trouble in the 1920s," Federal Bureau of Investigation, April 29, 2010, https://archives.fbi.gov/archives.

people or that [B]lack people's blood coagulates more quickly than white people's blood."[6]

Along with working to help people all over the country unlearn whitewashed American history, The 1619 Project also centered the work of contemporary Black writers, poets, academics, and novelists, including Eve L. Ewing, on the first African American poet; Jesmyn Ward, on the 1807 law that banned the importation of enslaved Africans; Jacqueline Woodson, on Sergeant Isaac Woodard, a World War II veteran who was the victim of a hate crime after his return home; and Yaa Gyasi, on the syphilis experiment performed by Tuskegee University on U.S. Black men in the early to mid-twentieth century. The project covered the Middle Passage, the route taken during the Atlantic slave trade from Africa to slaveholding countries such as Brazil, the Dominican Republic, and the United States; the Fugitive Slave Act of 1793, which returned to slaveholders an enslaved person who tried to escape; the New Orleans Massacre of 1866, a violent conflict between Black Republicans and white Democrats, which resulted in the deaths of forty-four Black people; the Black Panther Party; and Hurricane Katrina. The goal of the project, released four hundred years after enslaved Africans arrived in 1619 in what became Virginia, viewed by many as the start of American chattel slavery, was "to place the consequences of slavery and the contributions of [B]lack Americans at the very center of the story we tell ourselves about who we are as a country."[7] In 2020, Jones and her team won a Pulitzer Prize for Commentary for The 1619 Project.

---

6. Linda Villarosa, "Medical Inequality," in *The 1619 Project*, 57.
7. Jake Silverstein, "Editor's Note," in *The 1619 Project*, 5.

Catholic Education

This work challenged me to understand more deeply how U.S. chattel slavery has impacted Black Americans and to accept that much of what American textbooks taught me about U.S. history was wrong. Our educational system often serves as American propaganda, particularly with white teachers who continued to portray our nation not as the white supremacist oppressor that it is but as the true savior for marginalized groups from the days of slavery to the Trump administration. Textbooks used in American classrooms indoctrinate young girls and boys "with narratives more interested in emphasizing the compassion of enslavers than the cruelty endured by the enslaved," wrote writer and historian Cynthia Greenlee in 2019, adding, "Textbooks have long remained a battleground in which the humanity and status of [B]lack Americans have been contested. Pedagogy has always been preeminently political." The 1619 Project helped me to unlearn false histories and gave me a lens from which to critique more fully my Catholic education, as well as my church and its leaders; and to learn about the church's history with racism and the sin of slavery. Because of my reporting, I was familiar with recent racial justice efforts from the U.S. Conference of Catholic Bishops. For years, Black and Brown religious women and men have aligned themselves fully with the fight for racial justice, including Sister Patricia Chappell, a member of the Sisters of Notre Dame; the Rev. Bryan Massingale, a priest and theologian; and Sister Norma Pimentel, since 2004 the executive director of Catholic Charities of the Rio Grande Valley, who has been working at the U.S.–Mexico border. In 2017, the U.S. Conference of Catholic Bishops also formed the Ad Hoc Committee Against Racism to develop pastoral and political strategies to tackle racism in the United States; in 2018, the bishops published "Open Wide Our Hearts," their first pastoral letter on racism since 1979.

"Open Wide Our Hearts"

In November 2018, the American bishops' antiracism committee, which falls under the USCCB's Committee on Cultural Diversity in the Church, issued "Open Wide Our Hearts," which was the conference's first pastoral letter against racism since "Brothers and Sisters to Us" was published in 1979.

An official statement supported by *all* bishops but written by *some* bishops, this 2018 letter begins with a reflection of the ways that God's love unites us all. They referenced Pope Francis's reminder that "the salvation which God has wrought, and the Church joyfully proclaims, is for everyone. God has found a way to unite himself to every human being in every age." The statement included a relatively nuanced section on chattel slavery in the United States, a system in which "Africans were bought and sold as mere property, often beaten, raped, and literally worked to death." This inhuman treatment, the bishops wrote, was justified using "racial categories, which classified different ethnic communities as different races," adding that the "injustices of chattel slavery were horrifying and lasted for generations." These injustices included separating families and the mistreatment of children. Once slavery was abolished, the bishops noted, many freed Black Americans were forced into "continued servitude in the evolving economies that once relied upon their labor, and blacks encountered new forms of resentment and violence." They added that "most resided in extreme poverty and endured daily indignities in their interactions with whites. Efforts to advance out of poverty by working a small farm, owning a business, building a school, or forming a trade union generally met fierce resistance throughout the country. For so many, the right to participate in the political process would be withheld or severely hindered for another century." The bishops acknowledged that we were all living in a world full of "sin and death," and one of those sins was racism. This only existed, according to the bishops, because people of a given race have feelings of superiority over another, but they gave no explicit indication of which race demonstrated such feelings. These feelings cause racist individuals to discriminate against others, and, in turn, these racist actions are sinful because it leads certain races to deprive people of their human dignity and go against our Catholic commitment to justice. The letter calls on all Catholics, regardless of race, to work toward the eradication of racism in the United States.

Within "Open Wide Our Hearts," there is no mention of the Black Lives Matter movement or the work of Garza, Tometi, and Cullors. The bishops find time, though, to remind Catholics that we "must reject harsh rhetoric that belittles and dehumanizes law enforcement personnel who labor to keep our communities safe. We also condemn violent attacks against police." Two years later, however, in the summer of 2020, three U.S. bishops, including Archbishop Paul Coakley, chairman of the Committee on Domestic Justice and Human Development; Bishop Mario Dorsonville, chairman of the Committee on Migration; and Bishop Shelton J. Fabre, chairman of the Ad Hoc Committee Against Racism, released a statement calling for more accountability of police departments. They reminded Catholics that police officers must be committed to justice rather than power. They concluded their letter by supporting policy geared toward "[gathering] data on use-of-force, training towards de-escalation, work to end racial profiling, doing away with chokeholds, using body cameras, greater accountability and means of redress regarding those who exercise public authority, and a commission to study the issue further and make additional recommendations."[8] Such policies were necessary, the bishops believed, in order to prevent future tragedies at the hands of law enforcement.

My criticism of such rhetoric from church bishops, including its lack of action plans, is recorded in articles and tweets. However, there are two criticisms that are particularly important. The first criticism is the bishops' ahistorical representation of their role in the sin of slavery. I was familiar with some aspects of the church's history with slavery. I have read and written about documents such as *Dum diversas* and *In supremo apostolatus*. The first, a papal bull written by Pope Nicholas V, allowed "full and free power, through the Apostolic authority by this edict, to invade, conquer, fight, subjugate the Saracens and pagans, and other infidels and other enemies of Christ." In *In supremo*, issued by Pope Gregory XVI in 1839, twenty-six years before all enslaved Americans were free, the pope denounces both the slave trade and the continuance of the institution of slavery, calling bishops "to turn away the Faithful from the inhuman slave trade."[9]

I knew that religious orders, including the Jesuits, had started to apologize for the role in the selling and enslaving of Black Americans. In 2016, for example, Georgetown University, the oldest Catholic university in the United States, formed the Working Group on Slavery, Memory, and Reconciliation to present the university's history and ties to slavery. In 1838, the Maryland Province of the Society of Jesus, which founded

---

8 United States Bishops' Conference, "Letter to Senate on Police Reform," June 24, 2020, http://www.usccb.org.

9. Pope Gregory XVI, *In supremo apostolatus*, December 3, 1839, https://www.papalencyclicals.net/Greg16/g16sup.htm.

Georgetown, sold 272 men, women, and children whom it had earlier purchased as slaves. The working group published a report with recommendations for ways for the university to begin to atone for its slaveholding past that included renaming buildings and creating the Institute for the Study of Slavery and Its Legacies. John J. DeGioia, the president of Georgetown, announced that the school would also offer preferential admission to applicants who are direct descendants of the individuals the Jesuits sold.[10]

Nevertheless, I did not realize how deeply the Church's sin ran until I read the work of Shannen Dee Williams. She wrote that chattel slavery began not in 1619 but in the 1500s, adding that "the church served as the largest corporate slaveholder in the Americas, including Louisiana, Saint-Domingue (later Haiti) and Brazil."[11] As noted earlier, even when slavery was abolished, "most white Catholic religious orders of men and women and seminaries continued systemically excluding African-descended people, especially U.S.-born black people, from admission on the basis of race well into the 20th century."[12] The church took part in the terrorization that happened to Black people at the hands of white people who claimed to be Christians, who believed in a God-given right to oppress and murder. The church stood idly by as Black people were killed and terrorized by white Christians in the name of our faith. During the days of chattel slavery, church leaders took part in white supremacy, and this is a history that the American institutional

---

10. John J. DeGioia, "Next Steps on Slavery, Memory, and Reconciliation at Georgetown," Georgetown University, 2016, https://president.georgetown.edu.

11. Shannen Dee Williams, "Racism Has Always Been a Pro-Life Issue," The Pilot, July 12, 2020, https://www.thebostonpilot.com.

12. Williams, "Racism Has Always Been a Pro-Life Issue."

church has yet to grapple with. Not once in my Catholic education did I learn this, not even in a course I took in college on controversies throughout the church's history. I read Williams's research in June 2020, weeks after the George Floyd protests that same year. Along with our leaders' continued silence on BLM, they refused to authentically grapple with our church's complicity in the sin of slavery.

A second criticism is that the bishops, who chose to opine on police brutality, falsely equate justice with law enforcement. To equate justice with an American institution that Black Americans, including the faithful our leaders minister to, have repeatedly denounced as a violent threat to Black livelihood is a cruel failure on the part of the bishops, particularly in their role as spiritual leaders in the Catholic Church. The letter's vague policy demands further demonstrate how removed these leaders are from the organizers and policymakers who are calling for the abolition of U.S. police departments. By aligning law enforcement with justice and the fight for the "common good," the bishops are, once again, willfully ignoring the lived experience of Black Catholics. Rather than listening to Catholics of color who are traumatized by their experiences with U.S. law enforcement and calling for the abolition of police, the bishops in these documents, whether intentionally or unintentionally, feel less like pastors who are critically engaging with social issues and more like promoters of Catholic "copaganda," in other words, as supporters who "advance the narrative that police violence is an issue of individual bad cops as opposed to a systemic one, and minimize the very real violence and trauma police cause to Black communities."[13]

---

13. Palika Makam, "Copaganda: What It Is and How to Recognize It," *Teen Vogue*, August 5, 2020, https://www.teenvogue.com.

One of the biggest misconceptions I encounter in my reporting—by both white and nonwhite Catholics—is the idea that police departments are inherently moral and that their officers serve in the name of justice, regardless of skin color or race. This is both ahistorical and dangerous. The bishops, like the medical professionals who romanticize the work of men who experimented on Black people in the 1900s, must not contribute to the spread of fallacies regarding Black life. The bishops must cease affirming the very oppressors who are killing, harming, and harassing Black Americans. Our contemporary church fathers cannot disregard the violent history of policing any more than we can ignore the Catholic Church's role in American chattel slavery.

How can the bishops claim to understand that Black Americans have suffered for generations from various institutions born out of slavery but not be courageous enough to reject one of the most oppressive and violent institutions in the United States? Our church fathers must apologize for harming Black Americans, from the church's participation in slavery to its current alliance with police enforcement to its continued refusal to acknowledge the work of Garza, Tometi, and Cullors. If we are to be a universal church, then our church leaders must commit to a process of true and transformative accountability.

Transformative Justice

In *Beyond Survival: Strategies and Stories from the Transformative Justice Movement*, editors Leah Lakshmi Piepzna-Samarasinha and Ejeris Dixon provide readers interested in learning about the transformative justice movement with strategies centered around the needs and boundaries of victims of violence. The book features strategies from a variety of organizers, writers, activists, scholars, and thinkers, including Alexis

Pauline Gumbs, Amanda Aguilar Shank, Audrey Huntley, and Kai Cheng Thom. "The goal of transformative justice," Dixon writes, "is to find solutions for dealing with violence without the presence of law enforcement."[14] Such strategies include forming groups who will work with survivors of violence to decide what they want justice to be; providing safe spaces for women, men, and children escaping violence; and educating people about combating the prevalence of violence in marginalized communities.

I began applying this to the Catholic Church and our leaders. The pain caused by the church, as Williams's research proved, began with its participation in chattel slavery but continues, even into the twenty-first century, with actions like the church's repeated deference to law enforcement despite pleas from their Catholic communities of color. What would a Catholic transformative justice approach be in the fight for Black liberation?

First, our church fathers must address, through a formal pastoral letter, the harm that has been done to Black Americans by the Church and apologize for how the Church has been and continues to be complicit in white supremacy. We urge them to begin from a place of humility, from a place where they lay not just their physical bodies but also their spiritual bodies on the line for Catholics of color. In the pastoral, leaders can apologize for the pain inflicted on our communities, from the days of chattel slavery to the police murders of the twenty-first century; for the delays in response from our prolife bishops; and for the failures in ministering to us on a public level. True accountability requires the centering not of the church fathers or the most visible in our communities but those who are most ignored,

---

14. Ejeris Dixon and Leah Lakshmi Piepzna-Samarasinha (eds.), *Beyond Survival: Strategies and Stories from the Transformative Justice Movement* (Chico, CA: AK Press, 2020).

those who are most affected by unjust, white supremacist systems of oppression.

Second, the church must acknowledge the ways in which our church leaders, as a body of mostly white, male leaders, have benefited from privileges and resources not given to U.S. Black, ✓ Brown, and indigenous communities.

Third, our white bishops must ask themselves and publicly answer the following: Why does my white skin allow me to move through the world without a fear of authority? Why does my white skin allow me to cling to fables of officers fighting for justice and morality while being blinded to the brutality Black communities have faced for years? I implore white bishops to sit with their answers. And then demand that white Catholics, ✓ from priests to donors, do the same. Forget about losing money and resources. Remind these Catholics that *white* people created racism, and therefore they, *solely*, have a moral duty to work to abolish systems of oppression.

You, the church leaders, must work to keep Catholics of color, who have remained despite the humiliation, despite the ignorance, the pain. We remain because we have believed in a better, more liberated church than many of our church fathers can envision. For we are the faithful; we are the Catholics who lift and carry this institution, from the chains of slavery to border cages. We are the faces and bodies of Jesus. *Listen* to our cries and declare that the Catholic Church is committed to Black liberation—that Black lives matter.

Finally, tell us how, by centering the experiences of the most marginalized members in our church, you are going to build a church where white Catholics and church leaders denounce anything that belittles and dehumanizes Black people, who deserve to live safely; a space where bishops condemn violent attacks by police against Black bodies because Black Lives Matter.

Our bishops must be willing to reimagine a world in which white men and women, *regardless of money, status, power,* are held accountable. This is how we become a church that truly believes in Christ-centered, Black-centered liberation.

4

A Servant Leader

Tarana Burke, born in the Bronx, New York, in 1973, used to identify as Catholic. She was baptized as an infant and attended Catholic schools from first to eighth grade. Her Bronx home was an interfaith house where she was allowed to choose her religion. Burke's mother and brother were Muslim, and her grandfather was Christian, the latter introducing her to Catholicism. She internalized, at a young age, notions of compassion, grace, and service. It was the structure and rules of Catholicism that helped her to navigate life as a survivor after she was sexually assaulted—first as a young child and later as a teenager. Christianity helped her to feel that she had a place in the world and to see the ways God was moving inside her lived, traumatic experience. "As a survivor of sexual violence, Catholicism was a place, a way for me to gauge how to exist in the world," Burke told me in 2018.[1] "Inside of this trauma, there was hope. I don't have to have a way to show I'm actually good and not bad. I'm just following these rules." These rules that Burke described are rooted in Catholic social teaching, which teaches us that as Christians,

---

1. Olga Segura, "#MeToo Founder Tarana Burke: 'Jesus Was the First Activist that I Knew,'" *Sojourners*, September 24, 2018, https://sojo.net.

we are to care about our planet and the ways we have harmed it, prioritize the poorest and most marginalized in society, and respect the dignity of every human person. Humanity, as our U.S. faith leaders profess, is the very moral backbone of our country because each of us is sacred and made in the image of God. Burke's advocacy, like our faith, envisions a world where Black women and girls are free of the sexual violence that threatens the sanctity of Black life.

Burke began organizing as a teenager. After college, she moved to Selma, Alabama, and worked with a youth advocacy group called 21st Century. In this work, she often met young Black girls who were sexually assaulted but had no access to resources that were helpful for survivors.

In 2003, Burke founded Just Be Inc.[2] to help educate young girls about topics like consent, hair texture, and sexual assault. The goal of the organization was to provide young girls with the resources and tools to become women who know their worth and dignity. Three years later, she turned the "Me Too" training program under Just Be into its own organization. A young girl whom she met while counseling in the 1990s inspired the name. Burke described how she was initially apprehensive of the young girl's behavior and attempts to talk with her. Eventually, the young girl confided in her that her mother's partner was sexually assaulting her. Despite being a survivor herself, Burke, a young woman at the time, offered no solace and directed the young girl to another counselor:

> I watched her walk away from me as she tried to recap-
> ture her secrets and tuck them back into their hiding
> place. I watched her put her mask back on and go back

---

2. See https://justbeinc.wixsite.com/justbeinc/purpose-mission-and-vision.

into the world like she was all alone. I couldn't even bring myself to whisper, "me too."[3]

Me Too works to address the sexual violence that women of color, particularly Black women and girls, face in the United States, where every year, more than 500,000 people are sexually assaulted. Black and indigenous women are almost three times more likely than any other ethnicity to face sexual violence. Transgender people face disproportionate rates of sexual violence every year, and at least 47 percent have reported being sexually assaulted. Thirteen percent of transgender children (K–12) were sexually assaulted by classmates or school staff; 21 percent of transgender students in college have been victims of sexual violence; and 17 percent of transgender people who are experiencing homelessness face sexual violence in shelters. The goals of Me Too include highlighting the pandemic of sexual abuse that occurs within communities of color; providing survivors with the resources needed to heal; and helping to destigmatize the lived experiences of survivors. Burke's advocacy addresses the daily, often ignored, violence that threatens the lives of women of color. Like her faith, it centers on community, solidarity, and healing. "We are working across cultural lines; we're working together because regardless of what issue you're dealing with—sexual violence impacts it."

A Whitewashed Church Scandal

The summer before my conversation with Burke, the second round of the clerical sexual abuse crisis hit the Catholic Church. In July 2018, after a two-year investigation that looked into the dioceses of Erie, Greensburg, Harrisburg, Allentown, Scranton,

---

3. Tarana Burke, "The 'Me Too' Movement—Inception," Just Be Inc., https://justbeinc.wixsite.com.

and Pittsburgh, the office of the attorney general of Pennsylvania published a report, which found that more than three
hundred priests were credibly accused of abusing more than
one thousand children. Faith leaders in the United States and
the Vatican, the report alleged, systematically covered up this
abuse.[4] That same month, the *New York Times* broke the news
that then-Cardinal Theodore McCarrick, one of the most influ-
ential bishops in the American church, sexually assaulted male
minors and adult seminarians over decades. American bishops,
reports alleged, knew about McCarrick's sexual abuse as early
as 1993.[5]

I was too young to remember the first round of the clerical
abuse scandal in the early 2000s, my young mind unable to
understand how the faith of my childhood could be affected by
the actions of white men. My Catholic identity, at the time of
the first sexual abuse scandal in the church, had been formed
by my mother, Francisca, a devout, Catholic woman, who never
attends Mass but has an unshakeable relationship with Christ,
and by my father, who was raised Seventh-day Adventist and
currently identifies as an atheist. Like it was in Burke's home,
religious curiosity was encouraged but never enforced outside
of the requirements of our Catholic schools from first grade
through college; we were allowed to decide the role that faith
would play in our lives. Consequently, Pamela, my younger sister, was baptized, received the Eucharist, and was confirmed
in the seventh grade; she has since moved entirely away from
Catholicism. I have yet to be baptized, but the tenets of the

---

4. Office of Attorney General, "Report I of the 40th Statewide
Investigating Grand Jury," https://www.attorneygeneral.gov/report.

5. Laurie Goodstein and Sharon Otterman, "He Preyed on Men
Who Wanted to Be Priests. Then He Became a Cardinal," *New York
Times*, July 16, 2018, https://www.nytimes.com.

Catholic faith have informed everything that I do professionally and personally.

At the time of these scandals, I was one of the co-hosts of *Jesuitical*, a weekly podcast that featured our analysis of Catholic and secular news, guest interviews, and faith sharing. My co-hosts, producer, and I were trying to produce commentary that analyzed the second round of the clerical abuse crisis and centered the experiences of survivors. I was also familiarizing myself more fully with Burke's work and realized that these crises did not paint a fuller, more intersectional picture of our church. Marginalized communities were more vulnerable to sexual violence, especially against Black and indigenous women, yet most of the Catholic survivor stories that were getting covered were those of white survivors. One of the few mainstream media stories that featured Black survivors was published in 2018 and featured three victims who received significantly smaller settlement amounts than white victims. Advocacy organizations, like Survivors Network for those Abused by Priests (SNAP), which is a nonprofit advocacy group created in 1989, even have a difficult time getting Black survivors who are willing to share their stories. Yet Burke's work proved that Black victims were not an anomaly; they were, in fact, more susceptible to sexual violence than almost all ethnic groups, except indigenous women, but received very little emotional, financial, and restorative support—all crucial aspects of survival.

Burke's advocacy can help our mostly white, male faith leaders and other white Catholics to begin to dismantle their internalized, white supremacist Christianity. Her work is also a reminder to white Catholics committed to social justice that all efforts toward liberation must be centered on intersectionality, which is a term "coined in 1989 by professor Kimberlé Crenshaw to describe how race, class, gender, and other individual characteristics 'intersect' with one another and overlap."[6] Burke's advocacy is rooted in hope and possibility, tenets she internalized early through her association with Catholicism, and in her lived experience as a Black woman in the United States. Her work as an activist has, for over twenty years, been focused on what she described as the teachings of "Jesus the activist"; she tries to treat those she serves as Jesus would. Her leadership as a Christ-centered civil rights leader allows her to use her faith to achieve true healing and transformative justice, one that helps survivors figure out what *they* want justice to be. By the time I interviewed Burke, I had been reporting on the Black Lives Matter movement for years, and in a very specific Catholic, Jesuit context. The voices in both of these worlds introduced me to the concept of reimagining a better, more liberated church; but it was Burke who helped me to realize how my own understanding of Catholic social teaching could inform my reporting on liberation. Catholics can work to create a church that embraces the full holiness of *every* human person rather than just *white* women and men. This will teach our church to become one that is committed to being accessible, engaging, exciting—and *relevant*. Pope Francis talks often about what it means to be faithful and about the need to remember that we are all in the same church and should therefore have the same access to theology.[7] Everyone's words should matter in our church. We can use the resources of our faith to enter into an activist space using the doctrine and words of Jesus. White church leaders and Catholics can create a church where the oppressed can truly heal and be free, where they can truly repent and, eventually, stand in true allyship.

---

6. Jane Coaston, "The intersectionality wars," *Vox*, May 28, 2019, https://www.vox.com.

7. "Pope Francis Celebrates the Feast of the Ascension," Vatican Radio, May 28, 2017, http://www.archivioradiovaticana.va.

Burke's work went viral in 2017, using the hashtag #MeToo, when actress Alyssa Milano invited women to share their experiences of sexual harassment or abuse after women came forward in Hollywood and accused Harvey Weinstein of sexual abuse.[8] Milano invited survivors to share their stories of abuse or harassment on Twitter. The movement quickly became coopted by the faces of white celebrities, with many believing that Milano was the founder. As more and more white celebrities began to adopt the movement's rhetoric, more people failed to learn Me Too's history accurately and to credit Burke as its creator. Just a month before I spoke with Burke, I attended the Kent Ideas Festival in Kent, Connecticut, where paying attendees—almost all white—went to a variety of panels on topics including government, the Trump administration, technology, education, and psychedelics.[9] The panelists, many unknown to me except the *New York Times* writer Charles Blow, included Rana Foroohar, Fiona Donovan, Jay Kriegel, and Jessica Matthews. I attended an event on sexual harassment in the age of Me Too. None of the female panelists or the moderator mentioned Burke. I asked the civil rights activist how she felt about the first-year anniversary of her work going viral. Initially, she was not sure that the organization could function at the national level. So much of Burke's work has, for years, worked outside of any spotlight. It was her faith, she added, that helped to center her and remind her that the work is not about her but about the fight to eradicate sexual violence. "This work will never be about me. I'm in service to people, I'm in service to God, and that's what drives it."[10]

---

8. Alyssa Milano, https://twitter.com/alyssa_milano/status/9196 59438700670976?lang=en. See also CST, http://www.usccb.org.

9. Kent Presents 2018: A Festival of Ideas, https://kentpresents. org.

10. Segura, "#MeToo Founder Tarana Burke."

The Call for an Intersectional Church

Catholic social teaching is a crucial part of our faith. Inspired by Jesus's words and teachings, we are taught that human life is sacred, and that we are all part of one, collective human family. Catholics are called to fight for workers' rights, show preferential care for the impoverished, and protect the planet. We must work to promote "a fundamental right to life and a right to those things required for human decency. Corresponding to these rights are duties and responsibilities—to one another, to our families, and to the larger society."[11] The bishops include documents to help Catholics understand the foundations of Catholic social teaching, including *Rerum novarum, Pacem in terris, Deus caritas est*, and *Laudato si'*.[12] Catholic social teaching informed my vocation as a writer. At America Media, I first learned to read and interpret our church through its texts. For example, I read *Rerum novarum* in 2018. This encyclical, by Pope Leo XIII, was released on May 15, 1891. Leo criticized nineteenth-century socialism, promoted an individual's right to private property, criticized capitalism, and supported labor unions:

> It has come to pass that working men have been surrendered, isolated and helpless, to the hardheartedness of employers and the greed of unchecked competition. The mischief has been increased by rapacious usury, which,

---

11. USCCB, "Seven Themes of Catholic Social Teaching," in *Sharing Catholic Social Teaching: Challenges and Directions* (Washington, DC: USCCB, 1998), and *Faithful Citizenship: A Catholic Call to Political Responsibility* (Washington, DC: USCCB, 2003), http://www.usccb.org.

12. See USCCB, "Foundational Documents," 2020, http://www.usccb.org.

although more than once condemned by the Church, is nevertheless, under a different guise, but with like injustice, still practiced by covetous and grasping men. To this must be added that the hiring of labor and the conduct of trade are concentrated in the hands of comparatively few; so that a small number of very rich men have been able to lay upon the teeming masses of the laboring poor a yoke little better than that of slavery itself. (*RN*, 3)

When the Vatican published this encyclical, the United States had already abolished slavery, which gave birth to the very capitalism the bishops criticized. The encyclical, however, made no mention of racial capitalism or the ways in which it devastated nonwhite citizens, particularly in the United States. At the time of its publication, white Americans were experiencing tremendous economic growth through the expansion of technology. Such growth, however, exacerbated the post-slavery oppression of Black Americans, who were losing the miniscule rights they had achieved during the Reconstruction Era. This is because, as Cedric J. Robinson argues, capitalism has always been racialized to exploit nonwhite communities thanks to its roots in feudalism:

The bourgeoisie that led the development of capitalism were drawn from particular ethnic and cultural groups; the European proletariats and the mercenaries of the leading states from others; its peasants from still other cultures; and its slaves from entirely different worlds. The tendency of European civilization through capitalism was thus not to homogenize but to differentiate— to exaggerate regional, subcultural, and dialectical differences into "racial" ones. As the Slavs became the

natural slaves, the racially inferior stock for domination
and exploitation during the early Middle Ages, as the
Tartars came to occupy a similar position in the Ital-
ian cities of the late Middle Ages, so at the systemic
interlocking of capitalism in the sixteenth century, the
peoples of the Third World began to fill this expanding
category of a civilization reproduced by capitalism.[13]

Becoming an intersectional church meant our leaders must
publicly grapple with the concept of racial capitalism and its
continued devastation of marginalized communities.

The Congregation for Catholic Education (CCE) was first
established in 1588 under Pope Sixtus V. Four hundred years
later, in 1988, Pope John Paul II established the current iteration of the organization. For years, the CCE oversaw the management of male clergy around the world, but in 2013, Pope
Benedict XVI, along with giving the organization its current
name, shifted this oversight from the CCE to the Congregation
for the Clergy. The main goal of the organization is to supervise
Catholic schools and institutions around the world.[14] It also
publishes documents meant to guide lay people on issues in the
Zeitgeist. These documents are viewed as official church teaching. In 2008, the CCE published a document that described
homosexuality as a cause of immaturity in women and men.[15]

---

13. Cedric J. Robinson, *Black Marxism: The Making of the Black
Radical Tradition* (Chapel Hill, NC: University of North Carolina
Press, 2000), https://flexpub.com/preview/black-marxism.

14. Congregation for Catholic Education, http://www.educatio.
va.

15. Congregation for Catholic Education, "Guidelines for the
Use of Psychology in the Admission and Formation of Candidates
for the Priesthood," no. 10, June 28, 2008, www.vatican.va. See also

In 2019, the congregation released a document related to gender theory, which, it proclaims, "denies the difference of reciprocity in nature of a man and a woman and envisages a society without sexual differences, thereby eliminating the anthropological basis of the family."[16] Transgender women, men, and children, the Vatican believes, are incapable of developing fulfilling relationships. The document is important to highlight because it is a perfect example of the ways that church leaders, including Pope Francis, think about issues of sexuality and race. The document explores a topic that features only theologians, philosophers, and bishops talking about experiences they will never understand.

This is not Christianity. We are called to create spaces for the people who are the least among us, to fight for those who are oppressed, and to defend those who are most harmed by systems of oppression—regardless of whether or not we can relate to their experience. Jesus Christ did not teach us to be selective with our grace and mercy. If we are a church that constantly screams it is prolife, that it cares about human dignity, then we must care about the lives of transgender women, men, and children. I also quickly realized that the tenets of church teaching could be internalized by learning from movements, people, and spaces that were not Catholic. Thinkers like Robinson and women such as Burke are stronger examples of intersectional Christian witness than many bishops in our church, who often

---

Congregation for Catholic Education, "Instruction concerning the Criteria for the Discernment of Vocations with Regard to Persons with Homosexual Tendencies in View of Their Admission to the Seminary and to Holy Orders" (November 4, 2005): *AAS* 97 (2005), 1007–13.

16. Congregation for Catholic Education, "Male and Female He Created Them: Toward a Path of Dialogue on the Question of Gender Theory in Education," no. 2, June 10, 2019, www.vatican.va.

contribute to the daily violence faced by the most marginalized, particularly those in the LGBTQIA community.

As the Vatican proclaims that people who reject their natural birth are merely swinging between sexes to antagonize tradition, women of color face particular risks of violence in their everyday lives, from higher risks of domestic violence to higher maternal mortality rates.

I was also trying to figure out why I remained in a church that seemed to ignore the pain and trauma of Black communities. As mainstream media continued its coverage of the clerical abuse crisis in 2018, secular friends often added their thoughts, asking, more out of a voyeuristic curiosity than any actual concern for a church they mostly ignored, why I remained in a church full of abusers, liars, and racists. Not all priests, I often found myself saying, were evil. Some started organizations to introduce spirituality to those who were incarcerated; others used their public platforms to demand that church leaders and all Catholics create an LGBTQIA-friendly church; and some used theology to push white students past white fragility and discomfort. There were countless examples of strong, male Catholic witness beyond the bishops, but I still struggled, asking myself: Why did I stay? Why did I attach my identity to such an institution?

My conversation with Burke helped me realize that my denomination did not determine how I lived out my faith; it merely gave me the *language* to talk about why every person mattered; and why God called us to care for the planet. A true belief in these teachings has led so many white Catholics, particularly in 2020, to declare, finally, that Black lives matter and to stand behind the movement. My Catholic identity—my vocation—is tied to how I live out my commitment to creating a more Christ-centered, liberated world. To stop feeling desolate whenever white, male Christian leaders do not live up to their church positions and fail the faithful, I had to reimagine a theology that was centered not in whiteness, but in the Christian servitude of women like Burke, Alicia Garza, Opal Tometi, and Patrisse Cullors. To push our church into a truly reimagined and affirming space for all, our leaders need to understand that Black Lives Matter is not a movement pushing an extremist agenda that contradicts our faith; it is the secular version of Catholic social teaching.

Garza, Tometi, and Cullors, founded Black Lives Matter as "an ideological and political intervention in a world where Black lives are systematically and intentionally targeted for demise." They promote "an affirmation of Black folks' humanity, our contributions to this society, and our resilience in the face of deadly oppression."[17] These women called attention to the ways that Black lives were robbed of their *dignity* and *worth*; how white people often refused to stand in *solidarity* with Black communities, communities often most affected by the human *disregard for God's* creation—themes familiar to Catholics. Like our church, the movement places value on human beings, emphasizes building community and supporting one another against systems of racism and oppression, and centers the most vulnerable. However, Black Lives Matter and the movements and activists it has inspired are not afraid to align explicitly with the most marginalized—Black women and men and those in the queer and transgender community; the movement is courageous enough to understand why public acts of solidarity are the first step toward reconciliation.

Black Lives Matter takes the tenets of Catholic social teaching one step further by truly informing citizens how to prioritize human life and how to fight for Black liberation and dignity,

---

17. Cf. www.blacklivesmatter.com/herstory.

including resources on how to start local BLM chapters across the country.[18] The movement has helped to galvanize young people all across the country to take part in anticapitalist work, from marching, to book clubs, to raising money for the families of women and men killed by police officers or armed white vigilantes. They are engaging a demographic that the church desperately wants but seems unable, or unwilling, to relate to. Our bishops can learn from female activists who have used digital tools to get young minds engaged in Black liberation. In 2020, the movement also moved quickly to create policy and resources in response to the COVID-19 pandemic which disproportionately affected Black and Latino Americans. They provided information on requesting unemployment, on relief and loan grants, and on mental health services.[19]

By aligning ourselves with the Black Lives Matter movement and by using the tools of our faith in the fight for Black liberation, Catholics can work to create a church that embraces the full holiness of *every* human person rather than just *white* women and men. This will teach our church to become one that is committed to being accessible, engaging, exciting—and *relevant*. Most importantly, the BLM movement and activists like Burke remind us that as Catholics, to borrow Burke's words, we are called to serve. "I call myself a servant leader so that I don't ever forget that this is not about me, that this work will never be about me. I'm in service to people, I'm in service to God, and that's what drives it."[20]

---

18. See Movement for Black Lives, https://m4bl.org.

19. Black Lives Matter, "COVID-19 Resources," https://black livesmatter.com/covid-19-resources/.

20. Olga M. Segura, "#MeToo Founder Tarana Burke: 'Jesus Was the First Activist that I knew,'" *Sojourners*, September 24, 2018, www. sojo.net.

5

The Role of the U.S. Bishops

In *Freedom Is a Constant Struggle*, Angela Davis writes, "neoliberalism attempts to force people to think of themselves only in individual terms and not in collective terms." Throughout most of my life, I have internalized the belief that every American, regardless of race and class, has the opportunity to succeed in the United States. My generation has been told since our birth that, if we study and work hard enough, we too can build businesses or become billionaires. This is a lie, Davis writes. We chase after individualism, as Americans, and are left empty because racial capitalism exploits the work and subsequent failures of Black people, immigrants, working class, indigenous, Asian Americans, gay, lesbian, and transgender people, and countless other marginalized communities. Davis encourages citizens to reject the evils of capitalism and, instead, uplift our communities over our individual selves. She writes, "It is in collectivities that we find reservoirs of hope and optimism."[1] People, therefore, must actively and consistently work against the temptations of racial capitalism, an economic system that has exploited citizens

---

1. Angela Y. Davis, *Freedom Is a Constant Struggle: Ferguson, Palestine, and the Foundations of a Movement* (Chicago: Haymarket Books, 2016), 29.

around the world since chattel slavery, and focus on the needs of the community, the collective. Davis—a Marxist author, abolitionist, and feminist—was born in Birmingham, Alabama, in 1944. She was a member of the Black Panthers Party and taught at the University of California, Los Angeles, in the late 1960s. Her first book, *If They Come in the Morning: Voices of Resistance*,[2] was published in 1971. That was the same year Dorothy Day, founder of the Catholic Worker, called upon Catholics to engage critically with Davis's work, claiming that we cannot "prejudge her case any more than we can the case against Fathers Phil and Dan Berrigan."[3] In 1980 and 1984, Davis ran for president as a communist, a label that had gotten her fired from the university years earlier. For decades, the revolutionary has called for abolishing the American carceral state in our country and abroad, centered the experiences of queer and transgender people, and criticized the whitewashing of American feminism. Her advocacy has continually promoted the idea that it is in community and by being in solidarity with one another—including those who are being oppressed by American militarization in Palestine—that we will truly be free from the inequities caused by racial capitalism. Only by dismantling white supremacy on both a spiritual and national level, will we find freedom.

The Riverside Church

In September 2019, I heard Angela Davis speak at the Riverside Church, the Baptist church in Manhattan that I had been exclusively attending for over a year.[4] Having grown disillusioned

---

2. Angela Y. Davis, *If They Come in the Morning: Voices of Resistance* (Brooklyn, NY: Signet Books, 1971).

3. Dorothy Day. "On Pilgrimage," *Catholic Worker*, February 1971.

4. The Riverside Church and the National Conference of Black

with the Catholic Church and male priests, my husband and I attended several churches before Riverside, including a Pentecostal nondenominational one in Harlem where the people were friendly and intense. Many of the congregants were immensely faithful; many had overcome addiction, abuse, and familial trauma. I knew these stories because almost every Sunday people shared their conversion stories, their testimonies. These women and men taught me how to pray, how to turn my thoughts and emotions toward God, how to "pray without ceasing."

These spaces demanded a vulnerability I had never encountered in Catholic churches. Every Sunday after praying and worshiping, the community gathered and talked about the goals of the church, fundraising initiatives, and upcoming events the church was hosting around Harlem. Everyone in the evangelical congregation, around sixty or seventy people and their respective families, volunteered, led prayers, or babysat for fellow worshipers. They were all involved, from music to children's ministry. This was my first time in an evangelical space, and I found the immediate intimacy and theology confronting; but I craved the intimate Black and Brown space I encountered and the political and theological framework it forced me to develop. The pastor was unlike any preacher I had ever seen. He talked about revelations, prayed in tongues, and gave almost an hour-long sermon every Sunday. He talked about the perils of hell and the Book of Revelation. The end was near, he reminded his congregation often, and our entry into heaven was at stake. We were to forget about the temptations and concerns of our physical lives, including the antiracism protests we were seeing that summer because we were striving for something higher. These

---

Lawyers et al., "An Intergenerational Evening with Dr. Angela Y. Davis," September 23, 2019, https://www.youtube.com/watch?v= 0LHnZui1RMc.

spaces were challenging. It was the first time in my life when I was actively reading and trying to understand Scripture, something my husband had been doing all his life. I bought a Bible and attended Bible studies; the more I realized the other congregants' stances on issues such as homosexuality, reproductive justice, organizing, and gender roles, the more I wanted to try and use the Bible to refute their words. The downside of those intimate worship spaces is that people are not afraid to be overly familiar. I was asked questions about my living situation (at the time, my husband and I were dating and living together), my work ethic, my stance on children. They cited Scripture when attempting to persuade me that women were submissive to men and that marriage was strictly for heterosexual couples; yet when I read Jesus's words, I saw a Brown man who demanded we defend all LGBTQIA people. Christianity demanded that we be social, that we care about making a freer, more equitable world for our local communities and for those people and groups who are on the margins in the United States and the world. I know that following Christ means more than Bible recitations. The Christians in this community helped me to understand what I wanted from my church. I wanted spiritual pastors and spaces to fearlessly denounce systems that were killing and oppressing my people; I wanted a space where preachers, women and men, denounced white supremacy, racial capitalism, and violent politicians. I wanted my Christianity to teach me what it meant to dismantle systemic racism and work toward the bettering not of my own finances, career, and relationships, the goals I chased throughout my twenties, but the improvement of my communities. I was seeking a faith that would help me understand the anti-capitalist philosophies I was beginning to internalize. I would eventually leave the church after my husband and I were told that, in order to become members of the church, we had to sign a mission statement that stated that marriage was between a woman and a man and was meant to replicate the relationship between the Christian church and Jesus; and the Bible was infallible and to be taken literally.

We began attending Riverside sometime in 2018 and were familiar with the church's history with civil rights efforts and leaders, but it was the sermons that truly pulled us in. The pastors—men and women—were not afraid to criticize the American government and its leaders; they were not afraid to use Scripture to condemn racism, xenophobia, and demand that the most marginalized groups, the most oppressed, be given the power and resources they needed. They centered Black and Brown ministers and preached consistently about how the gospel demanded that we, as Christians, be anticapitalist, antiracist, and pro–gay rights. Their ministry included a Black Lives Matter chapter, prison accompaniment, and immigration resources, from lawyers to pastors who prayed and accompanied those facing deportations. Here was a space that was not afraid to chastise police and proclaim the names of those killed by state-sanctioned violence from the pulpit.

True Liberation

The event at which I heard Davis speak was hosted by the National Conference of Black Lawyers. As she has done for years, Davis touched on the ways that individualism has been conditioned into the psyche of every American. This is why, so often, many of us choose celebrity, status, and *individual* power instead of *community building.* True liberation, she told the audience, requires us to lose our self-conceit, which gets in the way of solidarity. We are unable to think globally, to think about the ways in which the violence we see at home is directly connected with the torture our government is committing abroad, especially in Palestine.

Along with rejecting the temptations of individualism, Davis called on citizens to broaden the ways that we all view what it means to be in community; we have to challenge constantly the systems and behaviors we are conditioned to view as integral to our safety and survival. "The work that we are doing at this moment is not just for ourselves—that's a capitalist idea that there is this immediate profit available," Davis said. "We're trying to create an arena that will allow us to constantly re-energize ourselves and those who come after us to do the work." In other words, we are to embrace not just the struggle for liberation but also the pleasure and joy we encounter along the way, feelings that make this fight for liberty sustainable. "We ought to be able to imagine ourselves being spiritually present over the years, the decades, the centuries."[5]

Her optimism was contagious. She was an atheistic revolutionary whose politics felt liberating and religious. The Jesuits taught me how to talk about discernment and what it means to understand the world around us, to see God at work. Davis directed those she influenced to look outward into the world—to be in community, to stand in solidarity internationally, and to understand that female oppression in Palestine is part of my struggle—that no one is free unless we are all free. Community building and organizing help us achieve generational liberation, one that is outside the constraints of racial capitalism. Davis was not strategically using religious rhetoric; she was speaking about a Black radical tradition most white Catholics and leaders in our church would shun; yet I could not help but hear her words from my Catholic context, one that needed broadening.

---

5. Riverside Church and National Conference of Black Lawyers et al., "An Intergenerational Evening."

Years ago, when I came across a copy of Davis's book *Are Prisons Obsolete?*,[6] which my sister had purchased, I found her work challenging and her politics divisive and, seemingly, at odds with my faith. The liberation she struggled for was too advanced for my thinking in my early to mid-twenties. I called myself a "liberal" but could rarely vocalize my ideas outside of familial settings; and even then, I was often yelling belligerently. I used every buzzword I saw on Twitter or in article headlines. I knew nothing about liberation, power, and community. As the 2020 global pandemic left countless in my community dead, jobless, or furloughed, and as antipolice protests erupted across the country, I found myself slipping deeper and deeper into anxiety-induced nihilism. I felt hopeless, rarely ate, and all my prayers felt empty. I wanted to silo myself away with my partner, my family, and close friends. For the first time in my adult life, I wanted to run away from the dangers of this country, this government, and our police force. Our leaders, church and state, were failing us, from President Trump's initial denial of the pandemic to the unwillingness of New York politicians to condemn the violence of the NYPD. So many of us became fully politicized that year. The American rich got richer, even during a global pandemic, thanks to racial capitalism. As 2020 progressed, however, and as I tried to write this book, I found myself returning to Davis's texts, particularly *Freedom Is a Constant Struggle*. She helped me realize two things: First, racial capitalism is not going to save us. There were 500,000 deaths worldwide in the first half of 2020; and once it became clear which communities were being disproportionately affected, the American government and many in mainstream media instantly changed their tone to focus on reopening the economy. Second,

---

6. Angela Y. Davis, *Are Prisons Obsolete?* (New York: Seven Stories Press, 2013).

socialism and communism are more compatible with Christianity than capitalism. Both mimic Jesus's commands: love your neighbor; dismantle oppressive institutions; give power to the weak. Socialism called for community, solidarity, power. This power, Davis taught, was centered on reimagining, as a collective, a world that allows every woman, man, and child to thrive, to prosper, to have power.

My parents, like countless immigrants before and after them, arrived in the United States in pursuit of a dream that told them they could get rich if they worked hard enough; yet despite working for over thirty years, they are nowhere near close to retirement. I am also living within this same system, one where women like me pay more than men for mortgages, lag behind men in retirement savings, and make up almost two-thirds of the student debt in the United States. We were never meant to succeed in this system. But what could replace the capitalism we know? What world could communities reimagine? How could I think about dismantling a system that created the very framework that has shaped my thinking since I arrived in America? The only way to dismantle a system that would willingly let thousands die, thinkers like Davis argued, was to organize as communities and take back our power. This involves allocating power and resources that require community organizing, one centered on the collective and not the individual. It was this work and the countless Black women and men whose names and faces many of us will not recognize that have kept the struggle going for generations. The work had to be done, Davis added at Riverside, even if we did not live to see it.

The goal, I realized, for those within and outside of the church, was to work toward this liberation, one in which all people are free. I have read secular thinkers who have described financial reparations as one way to repair the damage the United

States has caused African Americans, but it was not until I read the work of Kelly Brown Douglas, theologian, Episcopal priest, and author, that I had a theological context for reparations.[7] In "A Christian Call for Reparations," Douglas described a plan that Christian leaders must take toward repairing the harm they have caused Black Americans: become truth-tellers, develop moral clarity, and participate in public life. Faith leaders must be committed—as Davis also called upon Americans to do—to creating a freer world for future generations, adding that this effort "must be about more than compensatory reparations."[8]

The Church as an Active Presence

Let us now apply Douglas's brilliant, succinct, and theological framework for reparations to the Catholic hierarchy. We have already discussed in previous chapters the importance of retelling the history of Catholicism in the United States and the pastoral failures of church bishops. Here, we focus on how the U.S. bishops can use community organizing at the national level as a step toward reparations, which is discussed more fully in the next chapter.

Douglas writes, "If faith communities and institutions are to repair the breach between the unjust present and God's just future, then they must act proleptically; that is, as if that future is now. . . . This means that faith communities must be an active presence in the public square as sanctuary and witness." This presence requires that those who lead "make their spaces free of bigotry or intolerance, not simply in the most overt ways that these are expressed but also in the subtle ways that often

---

7. Kelly Brown Douglas, *Stand Your Ground: Black Bodies and the Justice of God* (Maryknoll, NY: Orbis Books, 2015).

8. Kelly Brown Douglas, "A Christian Call for Reparations," *Sojourners*, July 2020, https://sojo.net.

go unnoticed," adding that no one "should feel diminished or unsafe because of who they are or are not within a faith community or institution." Faith leaders must be the first to reject white supremacy and be willing to lead every effort "toward building a just society, thereby freeing the nation from its captivity to the sinful systemic, structural, cultural, and ideological legacy" of slavery.[9]

How can the bishops of the American Church work toward a more liberated world?

* * *

The U.S. Conference of Catholic Bishops was founded on July 1, 2001. The first iteration of the conference happened in 1917 when American bishops created the National Catholic War Council (NCWC), which was followed in 1922 by the National Catholic Welfare Conference. Forty-four years later, the U.S. Catholic Conference (USCC) and the National Conference of Catholic Bishops (NCCB) were created. These iterations became the USCCB. Since the early twentieth century, bishops have worked collectively, and often with lay Catholics, religious, and clergy, to address the social and political issues that affected the church and the United States. The goals of the USCCB are to work collectively and consistently on issues affecting the faithful in the United States; to maintain relations with church leaders around the world; and to provide resources to assist bishops in the overseeing of their respective jurisdictions. Every planning cycle, which lasts three years, the bishops supplement this mission with "priority goals." From 2017 to 2020, for example, the bishops focused on "mission responsibilities" and "mission relationships." Responsibilities include faith and morals; marriage

---

9. Douglas, "A Christian Call for Reparations."

and family life; vocations and church ministries; Catholic education/faith formation; the defense of human life and human rights; the promotion of human development and world peace; ecumenism; and prayer and worship. The U.S. bishops "jointly exercise certain pastoral functions for the Christian faithful of their territory in order to promote the greater good which the Church offers to humanity, especially through forms and programs of the apostolate fittingly adapted to the circumstances of time and place, according to the norm of law."[10] The mission statement assists the conference in its response to the problems happening across the country that demand "active leadership of the bishops," including "present needs or responsibilities for the Church in the United States" and national "specific responsibilities." The bishops collectively determine which social issues to address by selecting ones "that impact a sizable number of bishops and/or directly affect a number of dioceses." Once these crucial "issues and concerns" are identified, then the bishops must provide a "collective and unified response or approach from the episcopal conference." This means that bishops, appointed by the pope and responsible for the dioceses they oversee, must act collectively "to guide the church."

The majority of the conference, consisting of more than 400 bishops, including those in the U.S. Virgin Islands, are white. Less than 3 percent of U.S. bishops are Black.[11] In other words, the conference will not offer a position on something happening across the United States unless a "sizable number" of mostly white bishops are affected. This is why the conference and its previous iterations have released only four church documents

---

10. *Code of Canon Law: New English Translation* (translation of Codex Iuris Canonici) (Washington, DC: Canon Law Society of America, 2003), Can. 447.

11. USCCB, "Bishops and Diocese," 2020, http://www.usccb.org.

on racism, including two pastoral letters and two statements. The only collective efforts I have seen from the bishops are the formation of their antiracism committee and the pastoral letter "Open Wide Our Hearts: An Enduring Call to Love," issued in 2018. Individual bishops have released statements, including Archbishop Wilton Gregory and Bishop Edward Braxton, both of whom have written on the Black Lives Matter movement. In 2020, the bishops in Maryland wrote a statement that explicitly called out the "Church's past sins and failings" and acknowledged "that as Catholic leaders and as an institution we have, at times, not followed the Gospel to which we profess and have been too slow in correcting our shortcomings," adding that it was "incumbent upon us to place ourselves at the forefront of efforts to remove the inequalities and discrimination that are still present in Maryland and our nation today."[12]

Systems of Accountability

How can the U.S. bishops show Black people that they are genuinely listening and committed to the struggle for liberation? As Davis has taught for decades, they must work to free the church from the grips of racial capitalism. The church is an archaic institution, and working toward a church that is fully liberated and fully anti-capitalist will not happen overnight. However, if we are to prioritize creating a church that benefits not just Catholics in 2020, but future generations of the faithful, then we must begin to dismantle the white supremacy inside the Catholic Church. This means shifting our church from one centered on the power and leadership of a mostly white, all-male clergy

---

12. Archdiocese of Washington. "Building Bridges of Understanding and Hope: A Letter on Racial Justice from the Catholic Bishops of Maryland," June 15, 2020, https://adw.org.

to one that supports and encourages the teachings, desires, and concerns of Black women and men, and supports, both financially and pastorally, Black communities that have been most deprived by our nation's economic system. This is a call for creating immediate systems of accountability that guarantee that our faith leaders are listening and internalizing the experiences and demands of Black Catholics.

The initial steps of accountability and apology in this process are discussed in previous chapters. Calling upon bishops to organize as a community of church leaders builds on this work. Church leaders are disconnected from the faithful, particularly younger Catholics of color. Lay Catholics feel ignored; individual church fathers are speaking and writing the bare minimum. To change our church, there must be ongoing dialogue between bishops and Black Americans. Our church leaders must listen to the wants, needs, and demands of Black Catholics, a demographic our institutional church has harmed since the birth of the United States.

One way this might occur is through a survey. The USCCB could conduct a survey—possible platforms can include Google Forums, Survey Monkey, and Twitter Polls—to ask Black Catholics what topics they would like bishops to opine on as the pastoral leaders of the American church. How might this work? Before each bishops' conference, which happens twice a year, the USCCB could conduct a month-long survey to collect data on what issues Black Catholics want them to address. Suggestions might range from homilies on white privilege and antiblackness to pastoral letters on police brutality and abolition to fundraising initiatives. Once the submittal period is closed, the suggestions would be shared with the bishops before the conference. During the conference, the bishops, who vote on a variety of items during these gatherings, would discuss the top ten most suggested survey topics and then vote to write a brief pastoral letter—less than a thousand words—on each of the top three topics. The documents could be published on the official conference website and promoted on their social media accounts, which collectively reach more than 100,000 individuals. Regardless of the method, the goal is for our Catholic leaders to organize, atone, and internalize an ongoing, often difficult, journey toward a liberation most of us might never see. By also writing on the discussed topics, the conference of bishops would show Black and Brown communities that they are willing to give the dismantling of antiracism the same urgency they have given other prolife issues. Statements from the bishops, which often serve as the only time many Catholics can read how bishops are thinking on a given topic, can hopefully create a culture that enables the bishops to begin, as a group of mostly white men, to start thinking about the ways that their ministry and decisions as pastors are informed by their experiences as white, American men inside a very powerful church—a church that during an election year received continued attention from a white supremacist president, without any challenge from the *collective* body of bishops.

Throughout my years of reporting, I have talked to countless Black and Brown Catholics about what they want from their church fathers, and that I include in the final chapters of this book. The first response is often that we want a church that cares about us, one that actually listens. Rather than asking what the faithful want, our faith leaders at best, ignore our laments, and at worst, release statements that merely reinforce false white supremacist myths about Black communities. To repair this harm, the Catholic Church must listen to the Black women and men who are leading the efforts toward a more liberated and Christ-like world, from Christian thinkers like Kelly

Brown Douglas and Shannen Dee Williams to activists like Angela Davis, Alicia Garza, Patrisse Cullors, and Opal Tometi. The church must accept that it can no longer continue to cling to the evils of racial capitalism. Our Catholic bishops must actively work at being allies of Black leaders in the struggle for liberation, working against racial capitalism, organizing as a collective body of bishops to talk about topics that matter to Black communities, and making reparations to Black Americans.

6

Reparations and
the Catholic Church

Following the 2018 publication of "Open Wide Our Hearts," the USCCB's antiracism letter, I spoke with Leslye Colvin, the first Catholic woman to get me thinking about the concept of power. She told me that she had wished the bishops were courageous enough to talk about the power that fuels white privilege: the desire to control.

Since the days of chattel slavery, white Americans have received unearned social advantages that are not afforded to citizens of color. Furthermore, as we noted earlier, since America's birth, white Americans have always used the law to disadvantage Black Americans. As we have also noted, in the twenty-first century, there are tremendous disparities between white and Black lives in our country: Black women are more likely to die during childbirth than any other group; transgender women and men face higher rates of violence than any other demographic; and Black girls are more likely to get suspended and arrested in schools than white girls. In 2020, during the pandemic, Black people were more harassed by law enforcement than other groups, and as the pandemic progressed, they were being disproportionately killed off by the coronavirus. White men make more money than any other group and are overwhelmingly better represented in politics, academics, journalism, and Hollywood. We will never overcome such disparities, Leslye said, unless our faith leaders, along with white lay Catholics, comprehend and actively work to relinquish their power. White Americans, she proclaimed, have been indoctrinated to believe that it is their right to be superior to all other citizens, a bias that is often unconscious. White Catholics must call out and rebuke this power.

We spoke again in 2020, Leslye said that since the time she became a Catholic in the 1960s, the bishops have never collectively attempted to grapple with white privilege and power. She was born in Ozark, Alabama, in 1958 to Tom and Alma, who were both teachers at segregated schools. While most of her family was Protestant, several relatives, including her paternal aunt and grandparents, converted to Catholicism in the 1960s. In 1966, her parents began attending St. Columba Catholic Church in Dothan—the same year that Leslye was baptized. According to her, this church was one of the few white churches that accepted Black congregants at the time. She talked to me about what it was like to grow up in Alabama, where activists such as Rosa Parks and Martin Luther King Jr. marched. These activists, who visited her home state, informed her faith. She is grateful for the changes she has seen in the church but believes that the struggle for liberation is far from over. To be a resurrected church, she said, our faith leaders must begin to renounce their own power and listen to the wants, needs, and concerns of Black Catholics.

The Sin of Racism

In August 2017, the Unite the Right rally occurred in Charlottesville, Virginia. White supremacists marched through the city's streets. Some carried Confederate flags; many carried tiki torches. Some described themselves as "the face of American fascism"; others shouted, "Jews will not replace us." Almost all of their faces were uncovered. On the night of August 12, six white supremacists chased and assaulted a twenty-one-year-old Black man named DeAndre Harris; on that same day, a white supremacist ran his car over and killed thirty-two-year-old Heather Heyer, a white paralegal who attended an anti-racism protest march to counter that of the white supremacists. In response, the then-USCCB president, Cardinal Daniel DiNardo, wrote that these events "have exposed the extent to which the sin of racism continues to afflict our nation," and, with the bishops, he created the Ad Hoc Committee Against Racism, the USCCB's first antiracism group. DiNardo noted that the group was "wholly dedicated to engaging the Church and our society to work together in unity to challenge the sin of racism, to listen to persons who are suffering under this sin."[1]

The first man appointed to head the committee was the late Bishop George V. Murry, SJ, who eventually stepped down because he was battling leukemia. In May 2018, Bishop Shelton J. Fabre replaced Murry to become the group's chairman. Fabre, who serves as the head of the Diocese of Houma-Thibodaux, was born in 1963 in New Roads, Louisiana. At the age of twenty-six, he was ordained; he became the bishop of the diocese in 2013. Currently, he is one of just six active African American Catholic bishops.

According to Bishop Fabre, the American bishops have acknowledged "the reality of racism" for years and "responded in many ways both collectively and as individual member dioceses." He remarked that the Catholic Church has the necessary

---

1. USCCB, "U.S. Bishops Establish New Ad Hoc Committee Against Racism," August 23, 2017, http://www.usccb.org.

tools "from the gospel of Jesus Christ, from our Tradition, and from our official church teaching to instruct and assist those seeking a path toward healing and action," all of which guides the work of the antiracism group.

Between 2017 and 2018, the committee held listening sessions, organized an interfaith leadership conference, and invited Bryan Stephenson, attorney, author of *Just Mercy*, and the founder of the Equal Justice Initiative, to speak at the June 2018 bishops' gathering in Fort Lauderdale, Florida. As chairman of the group, Fabre told me that his work was to "explore how contemporary issues around race and racism relate to the gospel of Jesus Christ, the Christian experience, and our lives as Catholics." Collectively, the bishops hoped that this work could help Christians in the fight toward racial reconciliation. Fabre's task was also "to bring together the committee" and gather "ideas and impressions" from around the United States. His work is representative of "the committee and bishops in the broader community."

At their gathering in 2018, the U.S. bishops approved and published "Open Wide Our Hearts." The hope for the letter, according to Fabre, was that it would challenge Catholics to grapple with American racism. As noted earlier, some of the aforementioned failures of the pastoral document include an incorrect definition of racism, no mention of white supremacy, and no acknowledgment of the Black Lives Matter movement. For years, I have reported on the bishops' statements. These documents are important because they often serve as the only time people can learn the bishops' opinions on contemporary issues affecting our country. More often than not, however, the bishops either produce inadequate statements that can be extremely inaccessible and too theological. As we noted in the previous chapter, Catholic faith leaders must become more organized among themselves and listen to the wants and needs of Black Americans. How many bishops, for example, are aware that Catholics of color were disappointed with the church's antiracism efforts? Many Black Catholics I have interviewed since the letter's publication wish the bishops had done more. "Racism is a moral problem that requires a moral remedy—a transformation of the human heart—that impels us to act," the bishops wrote. They apologized for the church's failings to live Christ-like but made no mention of what these times are or the church's participation in chattel slavery. There was also no comment on capitalism and its role in the selling of Black women, men, and children. The bishops call on Catholics to engage with those who are unlike us and work to dismantle systemic oppression, yet they provide no concrete action plans or focus on any of the issues that are most devastating to marginalized communities. They concluded: "We call on everyone, especially all Christians and those of other faith traditions, to help repair the breach caused by racism, which damages the human family."

The Disconnect

Rebecca Christian, a thirty-one-year-old doula, born and raised in San Diego, California, has been Catholic her whole life. Growing up, she loved going to church and singing in church choirs. It was not until Rebecca was a teenager, however, that she developed her Christian identity. She attended Loyola Marymount in Los Angeles, where she took theology courses and met Catholic priests who helped inform her spirituality. She also joined Catholic Underground LA, an organization run by Franciscan Friars of the Renewal. Spiritually traditional, she loves the various devotions and traditions of our faith. She remains in our church despite its inability to actively and consistently guide

Catholics, like Rebecca, who look to the doctrines and leaders of our faith for guidance; despite this, she adds, our faith leaders are unwilling to learn about Black Lives Matter. "The cognitive dissonance surrounding our church's leadership regarding the harm it has caused Black and indigenous peoples for centuries and its link to our current crisis are absolutely infuriating," Rebecca said. "There is this subtextual, pernicious idea within the church that because we are the true faith and this world is not our home we can be selective about repairing the harm we have committed against real people in real time—I assume that it probably comes from our theology on suffering, but redemptive suffering is not a license to commit or excuse harm." She believes that while our bishops prioritize abortion, they do so without an intersectional lens that addresses the social, political, and economic factors that contribute to a woman's reproductive health and choices. She adds that the issues she wants faith leaders to grapple with include reproductive justice, bioethics, the church's participation in colonialism and systemic racism, and meaningful ministry for single Catholics. Until our leaders grapple with oppression within the church and Catholic complicity in white supremacy, Catholics like Rebecca will continue to feel a disconnect between the teachings of our faith and the actions of our bishops. During the first half of 2020, Rebecca went to Mass only two or three times over four months, finding solace instead in prayers like the Liturgy of the Hours. "I think God is truly calling us to rend our hearts, to root out idolatry right now," she said. "My relationship with God and the faith is just fine, but I do feel malcontent, a sort of tension with being in the public life of the church right now. It's uncomfortable to go to Mass, and it's awkward to publicly be a Black Catholic on social media right now, but I do draw strength from the examples of the saints who have gone through far tougher times than this." There is a disconnect between the bishops' efforts toward racial reconciliation and the desires and concerns of Black Catholics. Rather than releasing antiracism documents that are virtually ignored by all dioceses across America,[2] leaders must reject their internalized white supremacy.

In 2019, I reported for America Media on the Catholic response to the USCCB's 2018 racism statement. Fewer than 20 percent of parishes had engaged with the pastoral letter in any way. Reverend Bryan Massingale, a theologian, ethicist, and author of *Racial Justice and the Catholic Church*, told me that part of the reason the bishops fail at antiracism work is because our institutional church continues to define itself as a white, European church. Massingale was born in Wisconsin. He was ordained in the early 1980s and has since used his ministry to challenge U.S. Catholic faith leaders. In 2019, he told me that until the bishops reject their internalized biases and privilege, our church would never advance. The church must stop treating racism, he said, like an ad hoc issue. He was critical of the church's antiracism efforts and described the creation of the antiracism committee and the publication of the pastoral letter as a step back for our church. "Anything they say about race always has the comfort of white Catholics in mind. That white comfort sets the terms of Catholic engagement with the issue of race." The bishops are afraid to come to terms with terms like white privilege and white supremacy. Massingale pointed to the young people across the country who are engaging with systemic racism and actively working to dismantle it.

In an Op-Ed for *Teen Vogue*, Michael-Michelle Pratt described these young activists as the Trayvon Martin generation—indi-

---

2. Olga Segura, "I Reached Out to Every U.S. Diocese. Here Are the Ones Implementing the 2018 Pastoral Letter on Racism," November 21, 2019, https://www.americamagazine.org.

viduals born between 1995 and 2015. Pratt described what it was like to watch news coverage following the shooting death of the seventeen-year-old, recalling a conversation she had in the sixth grade with her mother: "I told her I was angry, but also very scared. I expressed that I had experienced racism before (mostly what I refer to as microaggression). I recalled all of the instances that she and my dad had recounted their experiences with racism. But I had never seen racism on such a large scale before." Pratt described her days online and how it introduced her to the works of Audre Lorde and bell hooks. She learned about feminism, intersectionality, misogynoir, and policing. Like many in her generation, Pratt used what she had learned online to get involved and to help those in her community engage with the various issues she was learning. Her generation, like the Black Lives Matter movement, embraced community building as the path toward liberation. "We were children when George Zimmerman's act of violence against Trayvon Martin went unpunished," Pratt wrote. "We have marched, reblogged, retweeted, organized, volunteered, and donated. We are adults, or almost adults, now. This is a boiling point and it's spilling over."[3]

A Question of Morality

Kelly Brown Douglas reminds Christians that reparations for the sin of slavery cannot be viewed solely through a financial lens. This sin, which continues to exploit, oppress, and kill Black Americans since the first captive Black people were brought to America, requires morality. This means actively and consistently rejecting whiteness: "Ecclesiastical institutions and faith com-

---

3. Michael-Michelle Pratt, "Growing Up Black between Trayvon Martin and George Floyd Has My Generation at a Boiling Point," *Teen Vogue*, June 5, 2020, https://www.teenvogue.com.

munities must lead the way toward claiming a moral identity by naming and freeing themselves from their own institutional realities of white privilege."[4] Our faith leaders, she proclaimed, must actively work to shed their whiteness, their *power,* and internalize the idea that choosing whiteness over fighting for the most marginalized is immoral. "For inasmuch as faith is about partnering with God to mend an unjust earth, and thus to move us toward a more just future, then faith communities by *definition* are accountable to that future."[5]

Thinkers like Davis, as noted in the previous chapter, along with the Jesuits who surrounded me in my professional life, gave me the skills to understand that the future for which we were fighting was one that we will most likely never see. Yet, despite this, we are responsible for reimagining a future centered on Black liberation. Faith leaders in particular, Douglas wrote, had a role to play in the struggle toward a liberated and more equitable world. According to Douglas, along with developing the morality needed to lead as ministers, Christian leaders must also give reparations, financial and spiritual.

An Unwillingness to Engage

On July 5, Spokane's bishop Thomas Daly released a statement in which he described feeling puzzled by a white Catholic's support of the Black Lives Matter movement "because the movement is in conflict with Church teaching regarding marriage, family and the sanctity of life." Daly added that he found it disturbing that BLM has not vocally condemned the recent violence that has torn apart so many cities. Catholics "need not stand with

---

4. Douglas, "A Christian Call for Reparations."
5. Ibid.

BLM to stand for Black lives."[6] Furthermore, Cardinal Dolan of
New York, in an Op-Ed that read as the finest example of pro-
police propaganda, romanticized law enforcement—despite the
continuous harassment that this same NYPD was disproportionately placing upon Black and Latino New Yorkers. Dolan
chose to equate the oppression of Black people with the valid
criticisms of police brutality. He wrote, "One of the tumors on
our beloved nation, past and present, is that we often target
African-Americans, profile them, caricature them, blame them
and suspect them as the cause of all evil and woe in society. That
is raw injustice. But for God's sake, let's not now, in a similar
way, stereotype the NYPD."[7]

These statements demonstrate how white supremacist thinking has been internalized by many church bishops. Lacking
the anticapitalist framework that is crucial for anti-racism to
work, such statements rely on stereotypes and fallacies about
law enforcement to undermine a pro-life movement. In addition
to making these inadequate statements, all the U.S. Catholic
bishops have demonstrated an unwillingness to engage with the
work of Garza, Tometi, and Cullors, the founders of the Black
Lives Matter movement. Until all bishops reject their anti-Black
sexism and engage with BLM and its founders, they will never
develop the morality that Douglas described is needed to repent
and repair the harm caused by slavery.

To actively refute the bishops' unwillingness to engage, we
must shift the centering without our church and faith. Douglas

6. Sarah Salvadore, "Spokane Bishop Criticizes Catholic Charities'
Leader on Racism Comments," *NCR*, July 8, 2020, https://www.
ncronline.org.

7. Timothy Cardinal Dolan, "For God's Sake, Stop Demonizing
the NYPD: Cardinal Dolan," Op-Ed, *New York Post*, July 1, 2020,
https://nypost.com.

describes the need for faith leaders to center the Black experiences as crucial for their spirituality and ultimate salvation. By rejecting white supremacy and actively working to repair the harm Christian institutions have done to Black Catholics, our leaders must, for the first time in the twenty-year history of the USCCB, work to become moral leaders.

For the Catholic Church to place itself within this struggle, it must make amends for the ways that it has harmed Black Americans since the birth of the United States. As noted earlier, Shannen Dee Williams has challenged many of us regarding the church's true role in chattel slavery. Along with slavery came racial capitalism, an economic system that relied on the exploitation, torture, rape, and often murder of Black and indigenous people throughout American history. As the first churches were being erected across the country, as Catholic schools were being created, including some of the oldest Jesuit colleges, this country was simultaneously viewing Black women and men as objects that would enhance profit. Our own church, which claims to internalize the gospel, enslaved Africans; our own church used Black women, men, and children to promote its own well-being and success over Black livelihood. Throughout the American church's history and well into the twentieth century, religious orders were also actively working to keep Black women and men out. Williams wrote that many Black women and men chose, instead, to start their own religious orders. Universities run by religious orders, like Georgetown University, were also complicit in racial capitalism. The Jesuits who ran Georgetown University in 1838, just forty-nine years after the first Catholic bishop in America founded it, sold 272 enslaved persons to avoid bankruptcy.[8] "Colonial academies were born in the slave economy,

---

8. Cf. Georgetown University, "History," http://slavery.george town.edu/history/.

and that same economy founded the expansion of the educational infrastructure in the early years of the United States."[9]

Onita Estes-Hicks understands this history well. A cradle Catholic, born in New Orleans in 1936, Onita has loved the church her whole life. Her family had ties to the Knights of Peter Claver, an organization for African American lay Catholics founded in 1909 by Father Conrad Friedrich Rebesher, and growing up, they often hosted priests to dinner. She was educated in Catholic schools and involved in the choir. In 2004, her family learned that her paternal great-great-grandparents, Nace and Biby Butler, and their children, were part of the 272 enslaved persons sold by Georgetown's Jesuits in 1838. "This breached our awareness of ourselves, who we were as Catholics," Onita told me. For years, her faith struggled to reconcile their faith within a church that sold their ancestors. It took fourteen years before her faith felt whole again; and this was thanks to Georgetown's efforts to reckon with its slaveholding past. "I came out with a deeper sense of what it meant to be a Catholic and also with a deeper sense of how Catholicism had failed us."

Georgetown is the first American Catholic institution to grapple with its slaveholding past and offer financial resources as part of that atonement. As DeGioia stated, the school is truly committed to reckoning with its past. By repairing their racist past, Georgetown is actively working to align the Catholic tradition with the struggle for liberation.

In order to make amends, our church must do the same. This can begin by publicly embracing BLM. Racial capitalism dictates the ways we define what it means to be a corporate body,

---

9. Craig Steven Wilder, "Sons from the Southward and Some from the West Indies," in *Slavery and the University: Histories and Legacies*, ed. Leslie M. Harris, James T. Campbell, and Alfred L. Brophy (Athens, GA: University of Georgia Press, 2019), 22.

an institution, or a professional. The American church has so fully internalized these white supremacist ideals, rationalizing a spiritual racism of its own, that it is unable to imagine our church as one centered in the struggle for liberation under the leadership of *Black women*.

The inability to acknowledge this work also continues to perpetuate systemic oppression and accentuates the hypocrisy of the church on the issue of racism. The various arguments that there is no need to expect more from the bishops comes from a privileged perspective, one shared by mostly white Catholics, and proves even more why bishops must demonstrate that they care about Black liberation. Catholics of color deserve to see leaders who are prioritizing *their* wants, needs, and concerns.

Black Catholics want to feel heard; they want a church that reflects and uplifts them toward liberation; a church that cares about their spiritual and physical lives—a church that atones.

Church reparation must also be financial. The finances of the USCCB are distributed into the following five funds. First, there is one for general operations, which is funded by "diocesan assessments, investment income, and other sources." This fund helps "finance the current operations of USCCB." Second, there is the building fund, which covers the conference's property and assets. This includes "land, buildings, furniture," the "St. John's staff houses," and "improvements to the Villa Stritch staff facilities in Rome." The fund also sets money aside for any "maintenance and improvements these properties might require." Third is the general reserve fund, which was created in 1993 to finance "sudden, unusual, ad hoc and/or short-term projects." The fourth fund, focused on catechism, was created in 1995 to provide resources "related to the publishing, sales promotion and distribution of the United States release of the *Catechism of the Catholic Church*. The fifth and final one, the quasi endowment

fund, was formed in 1997 "to supplement the diocesan assessments by applying an annual spending rate to use for current
operations."[10] Every year, the bishops meet and vote on their
annual budget. The total revenue for 2018 was $203,649,630,
with a deficit of $29,475,656. This budget was spread among
the funds listed above, including specific subcategories such as
$58,969,590 for policy activities. This category includes migra-
tion and refugee services, communications, Catholic education,
and prolife issues. If the church is to embrace anticapitalism,
which it must embrace in order to work toward a truly liberating
Catholicism, then our bishops could begin by allocating a fund
from their various collections toward a reparations fund for
some of the most impoverished Black communities across the
country. Not only would this fund allow the bishops to support
marginalized communities, it would actively move the bishops
away from a reliance on funds to support their own, sometimes
lavish, homes or needs. The faithful cannot hear our church
fathers when they sit so far removed from our daily, impoverished lives. The Jesuits taught me that to be a faith leader, one
must take vows to guarantee that the focus is on helping the
most marginalized and on living out one's vocation. All Jesuits
take vows of poverty.[11] This vow helps the brothers and priests
develop deeper empathy for the communities they serve. I know
Jesuits who are serving Black communities and promoting the
work of transgender Catholics. These are men who helped plant
the anticapitalist framework I would develop years later. They
have helped shape my faith as one centered not on money but on

---

10. See USCCB, "Consolidated Financial Statements with Supple
mental Schedules, December 31, 2018 and 2017," http://www.usccb.
org.

11. See https://jesuits.org/aboutus.

encountering and rejecting the temptations of capitalism. Our bishops should consider taking vows of poverty.

The current racial crisis in America, one that creates ripple effects in marginalized communities around the world, is a moral crisis that demand radical, transformative reparations.

7

Racial Capitalism

When I was eleven and in the seventh grade, my mother worked at a Bronx laundromat, the coolest place to my nine-year-old sister, Pamela, and me. There were toy claw machines, and on slow days, we were allowed to play with the wire laundry carts. One year, we were even allowed to sell school candy there. Pamela and I sat at the table closest to the door, and every time a customer walked in, we yelled, "Chocolate for sale!"

My last few months as an eleven-year-old were accompanied by a feeling I had not experienced since my prekindergarten days: I was constantly anxious, convinced that my parents were going to die while I was in school. Most days I hid these feelings from my parents, or so I believed at the time; other days, I broke down sobbing, forcing my parents to keep me home from school. Since my father worked at his office at the time, I went with my mother to the laundromat. I knew that she talked to my father several times throughout the day; if I was by her side, I could watch and keep them both safe.

One morning, I sat next to my mom as she folded the clothes of a customer who paid for drop-off laundering services. The phone rang. I listened as she talked to my father. "*¿Que? Un accidente en las torres gemelas?*" I followed her as she walked to the television that hung in front of the store near the toy and vending

97

machines. I heard my mom describe to my father the plane crash that was being televised on the screen in real time. As she continued watching the news, I stared out the storefront. *It was so sunny,* I thought, *it was so unfair that we have to go to school, and school doesn't feel good.* The only other customer in the store stood next to my mother; they both looked serious and concerned in a way I only saw on adult faces. My mother called my father once again, and I heard her say: "*Un avión le doy a la segunda torre.*" A second plane had crashed into the second tower of the World Trade Center. Once we learned that there were two other attacks that day, my dad instructed us to pick my sister up from school. I cannot remember if my mother closed the laundromat or if I went with my uncle to get Pam, but I remember that the school was chaotic. Parents were picking up their children; teachers and students were worrying over parents, sisters, partners, cousins, and friends, all of whom worked in the city—what outer borough New Yorkers called Manhattan. Growing up, Manhattan had always been a far-away place that we frequented only when relatives were visiting from the Dominican Republic. It felt foreign to the Bronx I knew; yet, on that day, it became an inextricable part of my adolescence. I began to internalize the responses I was hearing from news outlets and celebrities following the terrorist attacks on September 11, 2001. My family came to the United States to be free, to work hard, and to build a home for our relatives. There were people out there who would kill as many Americans as possible in order to destroy our democracy and steal our liberties. We did not need to worry, however, because America, a nation founded on morality, dignity, and freedom, would use everything in its power, including its military, to keep the people I loved alive and free.

I heard this paternalistic rhetoric everywhere, from hip-hop stations to television shows. That morning, life as we knew it stopped: schools were closed; trains shut down; families across New York City sheltered in place. Gone were the noises made by children playing, ice-cream truck melodies, and basketballs bouncing—sounds that were normally heard all over New York well into October. One morning, I saw a firefighter who had walked from the D-train's Bedford Park stop to the fire station near my family's apartment. I had never seen such a look of shock on an adult's face until then. Later that same day, as we watched images of people in Manhattan running for shelter during the attacks, I was reprimanded by my parents for telling my sister that World War III was going to begin that very month. Shortly after, our parents limited our screen time.

Two months later, on November 12, another plane came down on its way to the Dominican Republic. The flight, which crashed due to mechanical problems, was familiar to the many Dominicans who traveled regularly to and from the United States. For years, every time I went to my hair stylist, who was a close friend of my mom, I would listen to stories from Dominican women about people they knew who had died.

Like many New Yorkers—and other Americans—we soon became conditioned to fear the worst, to suspect the *other*. Following the 9/11 attacks, President George W. Bush announced, "Our way of life, our very freedom came under attack in a series of deliberate and deadly terrorist attacks." The victims, he declared, were everyday Americans, like my sister, our parents, and me. His words reinforced the anxieties and fears with which I struggled. At the time, the president, I thought, wanted to protect my parents; they were the center of my world and he cared about that. The American president, to my young eyes, exuded leadership, poise, and strength. "Moms and dads, friends and neighbors, thousands of lives were suddenly ended by evil, despicable acts of terror," Bush told us. The lives lost and the subsequent "pictures of airplanes flying into buildings, fires burning, huge structures collapsing" caused Americans to feel "terrible sadness, and a quiet, unyielding anger." Almost three thousand citizens were killed during the attacks on September 11.

My country and its leaders were introducing me to names and places I had never heard of, while simultaneously giving me the political rhetoric to view these communities through a white supremacist lens. I heard such names as Osama Bin Laden and Saddam Hussein, and learned of the Middle East.

In a post-9/11 world, President Bush reminded the American people that we had the strongest military in the world, one that, if necessary, would gather more resources and get even stronger. It was prepared and extremely powerful. My faith, however, taught me that killing was evil, but here was my president telling me that it was okay because he was doing it for families like mine. Furthermore, he stated that soldiers would only kill "those who are behind these evil acts."

To my young, whitewashed mind, Bush seemed like Jesus, fighting against evil and in the name of the most marginalized, "the children whose worlds have been shattered, for all whose sense of safety and security has been threatened."[1] He was a prayerful man, and so I prayed for him. That same year, I recall that my seventh-grade teacher, one of just a few white teachers I had prior to high school, would punish his students by alternating between forcing them to stand in the back of the class while it was in session and writing a psalm of his choosing at least one hundred times on loose leaf pages. One incident that most angered the teacher was when a student, during a class assignment, painted Jesus as Black instead of white. My classmate was

---

1. George W. Bush, "Presidential Address," C-Span, September 11, 2001, https://www.c-span.org/video/?165970-1/presidential-address.

punished because, according to my teacher, depicting Jesus as anything other than white was wrong. Like Bush, he used faith to either intentionally or unintentionally promote the racism that has been in our nation since its founding; like Bush, he used that faith to justify punitive actions. That year, not yet able to engage with various ideologies without internalizing them, I learned, thanks to certain secular and Catholic voices I heard, that faith was selective; there were "good" and "bad" people. If you followed the gospel and America's laws, then you would avoid unjust policing, become successful, and build a happy and safe home for your family. If you followed the rules, then the United States of America, like its founders, would guarantee your success.

The Reality of a Pandemic

Nineteen years later, as the COVID-19 pandemic was ravaging the United States, I was nostalgic for those days following 9/11, when I believed that all our political leaders were moral, when I believed in the promises of racial capitalism—an economic system that played a huge role in 2020.

On December 31, 2019, the Chinese office of the World Health Organization (WHO) "picked up a media statement by the Wuhan Municipal Health Commission from their website on cases of 'viral pneumonia' in Wuhan." A day later, the WHO began an emergency response that "activated its Incident Management Support Team." This group ensures that the WHO deals with emergencies around the world adequately. By January 5, the organization had warned all its "member states," which included the United States; and on January 11, the first COVID-19 death was confirmed. Ten days later, the United States confirmed its first case. At the World Economic Forum in

Davos a day later, President Donald Trump made his first public statement on the novel coronavirus: "We have it totally under control. It's one person coming in from China, and we have it under control." By January 30, the WHO declared a global health emergency. The first person in the United States died from the coronavirus on February 6. Twenty-two days later, on February 28, during a rally in South Carolina, the president stated that the Democratic Party was "politicizing the coronavirus," which he repeatedly denounced as a hoax. By March 11, the WHO declared a global pandemic.[2] By April, more than two million cases had been confirmed worldwide, and more than 200,000 deaths reported; by July 1, the number of deaths would increase to more than half a million worldwide.[3]

In the United States, a large majority of deaths due to the pandemic were in Black and Latino communities. A huge factor in these statistics, according to sociologist Whitney Pirtle, was racial capitalism. Blacks and Latinos across America were facing "capitalist and racist systems that continue to devalue and harm their lives, even within newer, supposedly deracialized neoliberal agendas."[4] Across the country, these communities were dying at twice the rate of white citizens. Additionally, from February to May, the number of unemployed Americans grew by 44 percent—from 6.2 million to 14 million.[5] The ensu-

---

2. World Health Organization, "Timeline of WHO's Response to COVID-19," June 29, 2020, https://www.who.int.

3. Centers for Disease Control and Prevention, "Cases and Deaths in the U.S.," July 8, 2020, https://www.cdc.gov.

4. Whitney N. Laster Pirtle, "Racial Capitalism: A Fundamental Cause of Novel Coronavirus (COVID-19) Pandemic Inequities in the United States," *Health Education and Behavior* 47, no. 4 (2020): 504–508.

5. Rakesh Kochhar, "Unemployment Rose Higher in Three Months

ing fear and paranoia led to a rise in hate crimes against Asian Americans, sentiments that were repeatedly fueled by the Trump administration. As the global pandemic progressed, along with increased attacks against the Asian community, Black Americans continued to face harassment and death at the hands of law enforcement and armed white vigilantes.

On Memorial Day, a police officer in Minnesota arrested George Floyd. The white police officer pinned the forty-six-year-old Black father to the ground and firmly placed his knee on his neck for almost eight minutes. Repeatedly, as he was dying, Floyd cried out, "I can't breathe." Sixteen-year-old Darnella Frazier recorded the murder, and the footage quickly went viral on social media. Four days later, the police officer, along with three others, was fired. Protests demanding justice for Floyd and other victims lost to violence that year erupted across the nation. For months, protestors and organizers rallied. Corporations and celebrities, many for the first time, began to align themselves with the universal rallying cry for a safer and freer world: "Black Lives Matter." For the first time since the movement's birth, 60 percent of Americans supported the movement.[6]

Marginalized Communities

I was working on this book when New York was ordered to shelter in place. For weeks, my husband and I worked in close quarters, oscillating, like most Americans, from one emotional

of COVID-19 Than It Did in Two Years of the Great Recession," Pew Research Center, June 11, 2020, https://www.pewresearch.org.

6. Monica Anderson, Kim Parker, and Juliana Menasce Horowitz, "Amid Protests, Majorities Across Racial and Ethnic Groups Express Support for the Black Lives Matter Movement," Pew Research Center, June 12, 2020, https://www.pewsocialtrends.org.

extreme to another. A month into quarantine, both our fathers got sick and would remain sick for most of April. Testing, at that point, was next to impossible for people of most nonwhite communities. My father was unable to get tested for weeks because his symptoms, he was told, were not serious enough. These were not anomalies. The relatives of friends were repeatedly turned away from hospitals as our health-care system crumbled. "The mounting carnage in Trump's America did not have to happen to the extent that it has. COVID-19 testing remains maddeningly inconsistent and unavailable, with access breaking down along the predictable lines," wrote Keeanga-Yamahtta Taylor. "In ZIP Codes with a higher number of unemployed and uninsured residents, there were fewer tests. Taken together, testing in higher-income neighborhoods is six times greater than it is in poorer neighborhoods."[7] As American deaths hit 25,000, the president released guidelines on reopening the economy. By early May, he described his pandemic response as successful. Weeks later, Congress approved $669 billion for the Paycheck Protection Program, which was "a loan designed to provide a direct incentive for small businesses to keep their workers on the payroll."[8] The U.S. Small Business Administration stated that small businesses, which included companies with more than five hundred employees, could also be forgiven for these loans if "the funds are used for payroll costs, interest on mortgages, rent, and utilities." Some of the recipients of the loan included Church of Scientology branches across the country,[9] which received

---

7. Keeanga-Yamahtta Taylor, "The Black Plague," *New Yorker*, April 16, 2020, https://www.newyorker.com.

8. U.S. Small Business Association, "Paycheck Protection Program Loan Information," https://www.sba.gov.

9. Rachel Olding, "Church of Scientology Received Coronavirus Small Biz Loan from Trump Admin," *The Daily Beast*, July 8, 2020, https://www.thedailybeast.com.

between $150,000 and $300,000; Kanye West, who received $2,000,000 for his company Yeezus, LLC, which, in 2019, was valued at more than one billion dollars;[10] and U.S. Catholic dioceses across the country, which received an estimated $1.4 billion.[11] While people in my community were facing tragedy and feared getting sick, the rich got richer; and even during a pandemic that left thousands dead in under six months, racial capitalism was exploiting marginalized communities.

During this time, the USCCB released resources for priests who were ministering remotely, provided links for people to tune into online Masses around the world, and created resources for social media. On the USCCB blog, "To Go Forth," there were articles addressing the inequalities of the pandemic and how Catholics could get involved to combat the racial disparities in COVID-19 cases.[12] On March 13, in a statement on the coronavirus, Archbishop José H. Gomez of Los Angeles, the president of the USCCB, wrote: "We are confronted once more with the fragility of our lives, and again we are reminded of our common humanity; that the peoples of this world are our brothers and sisters, that we are all one family under God."[13] On May 4, almost two months later, Shelton J. Fabre, bishop of the Diocese of Houma-Thibodaux, along with Archbishop Paul S. Coakley, Archbishop Nelson J. Perez, and Bishop

---

10. Elana Lyn Gross, "Billionaire Kanye West's Yeezy Received A Multimillion-Dollar PPP," *Forbes*, July 6, 2020, https://www.forbes.com.

11. Reese Dunklin and Michael Rezendes, "U.S. Catholic Church Received Billions in Taxpayer Funds from Paycheck Protection Program," *Time*, July 10, 2020, https://time.com.

12. USCCB, "Resources for Catholics during COVID-19," http://www.usccb.org.

13. USCCB, "USCCB Statements on Coronavirus (COVID-19)," http://www.usccb.org.

Joseph N. Perry, released a statement on the impact of the pandemic on African Americans: "We raise our voices to urge state and national leaders to examine the generational and systemic structural conditions that make the new coronavirus especially deadly to African American communities. We stand in support of all communities struggling under the weight of the impact this virus has had not only on their physical health, but on their livelihoods, especially front line medical and sanitation workers, public safety officers, and those in the service industry. We are praying fervently for an end to the pandemic, and for physical health for all, and emotional healing amongst all who have lost loved ones."[14] A day later, Fabre and Perez, along with Bishop Oscar A. Solis, released a statement condemning the xenophobic attacks against Asian Americans. They pointed Catholics to the conference's 2018 pastoral letter on racism and reminded "fellow Christians and all people of good will to help stop all racially motivated discriminatory actions and attitudes, for they are attacks against human life and dignity and are contrary to Gospel values."[15] By the end of that month, Fabre would add to his public statements following the death of Floyd. On May 29, Fabre and six other bishops, including Perez, Coakley, Archbishop Joseph F. Naumann, Bishop Joseph C. Bambera, Bishop David G. O'Connell, and Bishop Joseph N. Perry, wrote the closest words we have received from bishops, collectively, aligning with the sentiments of the Black Lives Matter movement:

14. USCCB, "U.S. Bishop Chairmen Issue Statement Urging State and National Leaders to Examine Impact of COVID-19 Virus on African American Communities," May 4, 2020, http://www.usccb.org.

15. USCCB, "Bishop Chairmen Condemn Racism and Xenophobia in the Context of the Coronavirus Pandemic," May 5, 2020, http://www.usccb.org.

Racism is not a thing of the past or simply a throwaway political issue to be bandied about when convenient. It is a real and present danger that must be met head on. As members of the Church, we must stand for the more difficult right and just actions instead of the easy wrongs of indifference. While it is expected that we will plead for peaceful non-violent protests, and we certainly do, we also stand in passionate support of communities that are understandably outraged.[16]

Marginalized communities across the country were being ignored, the bishops stated, "and we are not doing enough to point out that this deadly treatment is antithetical to the Gospel of Life." Two days later, Archbishop José H. Gomez, the USCCB president, released his own statement, in which he condemned the death of George Floyd and prayed for his family:

The cruelty and violence he suffered does not reflect on the majority of good men and women in law enforcement, who carry out their duties with honor. We know that and we trust that civil authorities will investigate his killing carefully and make sure those responsible are held accountable.

We should all understand that the protests we are seeing in our cities reflect the justified frustration and anger of millions of our brothers and sisters who even today experience humiliation, indignity, and unequal opportunity only because of their race or the color of their skin. It should not be this way in America. Racism has been tolerated for far too long in our way of life.

---

16. USCCB, "Statement of the U.S. Bishop Chairmen in Wake of Death of George Floyd and National Protests," May 29, 2020, http://www.usccb.org.

How were women of color, I wondered, processing such a year? Our secular and faith leaders flailed as they tried to minister in a pandemic world that was also dealing with antiracist protests erupting across the country. Churches and communal gatherings were prohibited for months. Every communal outlet we had was replaced by digital platforms, which became more superficial than intimate. I talked to women both within and outside of the Catholic Church. Many felt as if they had no spiritual homes, while others were grateful to create their own female-only worship spaces. Others told me that the events of the year just confirmed what they had been discerning for years. For some, this meant they would not have children; others told me they refused to raise Black children in a country that valued money more than humanity.

One woman in particular, Clarissa Brooks, a Black, queer writer and activist, truly pushed me to internalize the message that capitalism was violence. I had interviewed her for an article on capitalism I was writing before the pandemic hit. The article was eventually killed, but Brooks's words challenged me. Like Davis, Brooks spoke of the dangers of neoliberalism and individualistic greed. "I don't want a world where I'm only successful. I want a world without oppression and that takes letting go of ideas around dreams that only involve myself." She helped me to detach myself from the paternalism I had internalized almost twenty years ago.

An Unjust Economic System

America is currently not a country that cares to protect women and men who look like my family, as I had thought back in 2001. Our entire economic system was created to watch people like us—immigrants, Black, *other*—fail. Capitalism has created the very world in which white people have made millions in the cannabis industry, while Black women and men serve time for weed possession; where working-class people have labored in toxic workplaces, while politicians and CEOs used the pandemic to get richer. Racial capitalism created the very world in which my Black father—who previously worked as a truck driver and often delivered to and from Amazon factories along the northeast—was forced to choose his health over work, while white men, such as Jeff Bezos, added more than $20 billion to their net worth in 2020 alone.[17] This is because racial capitalism in America creates a world in which "those with high socioeconomic status secure a superior set of knowledge, power, money, power, prestige, and beneficial social connections, all of which can alleviate the consequences of the disease."[18] From the pandemic to the antiracism rebellion, white men who had been elected to govern fueled the violence and death of that year by using white supremacist rhetoric to justify the disproportionate deaths of Black and Latino citizens. Trey Hollingsworth, a U.S. representative in Indiana, said that "it is always the American government's position to say, in the choice between the loss of our way of life as Americans and the loss of life, as American lives, we have to always choose the latter."[19] The lieutenant governor of Texas, Dan Patrick, said during a Fox News interview, "There are more important things than living. And that's saving this country for my children and my grandchildren and saving this country for all of us."[20]

---

17. Kenya Evelyn, "Amazon CEO Jeff Bezos Grows Fortune by $24bn amid Coronavirus Pandemic," *The Guardian*, April 15, 2020, https://www.theguardian.com.

18. Pirtle, "Racial Capitalism."

19. "Trey Hollingsworth: We Have to Get Americans Back to Work," WIBC, April 14, 2020, https://www.wibc.com.

20. FoxNews, "Lt. Gov. Patrick Responds to Backlash from

President Trump, like these men and like President Bush twenty years ago, actively worked to manipulate how the American people perceived the realities of their respective situations. For example, on May 5, Trump stated that while the American people were "warriors," people were going to die. However, he added, "we have to get our country opened and we have to get it open soon."[21] By July 6, five months after the first U.S. COVID-19 case was confirmed, more than 130,000 Americans had died.[22]

'Tucker Carlson Tonight' Comments," YouTube.com, April 20, 2020, https://www.youtube.com.

21. Bloomberg Politics, "Trump: We Have to Open Our Country," YouTube.com, May 5, 2020, https://www.youtube.com.

22. Centers for Disease Control and Prevention, "Cases and Deaths in the U.S.," July 10, 2020, https://www.cdc.gov.

8

A Liberated and Resurrected Church

"Resurrection meant that death would not be the last word, that slavery would not be the last word," writes M. Shawn Copeland.[1] Copeland, an author, systematic theologian, and the first African American president of the Catholic Theological Society of America, is one of the most prolific Catholic voices today. The former nun was born in August 1947, in Detroit, Michigan. Throughout her career, she has used her vocation to center the Black Catholic experience; her scholarship consistently challenges white Catholics to grapple with antiblackness in the Catholic Church. She has written about violence against African American women, the history of Black Catholicism in the United States, Black theology, and the role of Christianity in dismantling oppression. In her third book, *Knowing Christ Crucified*, Copeland writes, "Theology cannot, *must not*, remain silent or complicit before the suffering of a crucified world and the suffering of God's crucified peoples."[2] The role of theology, she argues, is to help us think and work to combat white supremacy.

---

1. M. Shawn Copeland, *Knowing Christ Crucified: The Witness of African-American Religious Experience* (Maryknoll, NY: Orbis Books, 2018), 35.

2. Ibid., xxv.

Furthermore, Jesus on the cross can help us to understand more deeply the violence enacted upon Black and indigenous Americans, and by extension other vulnerable groups around the world, throughout this country's history, from the slave codes laws, to American police brutality, to drone attacks, which have killed thousands in the Middle East.

Theology helps Catholics understand the ways that we are meant to work and struggle for a more liberated world, a truly resurrected world. Copeland writes, "The power of God in the cross was the power to live and to love—even when violence does its worst."[3] Christ rose from the dead, a crucial principle of the Catholic faith, and in his rising, Copeland argues, he showed us that our faith, one truly centered in his words and actions, was synonymous with liberation.

All the violence of our current world, which belief in the resurrection actively and consistently rejects, was caused by the white supremacist need to dominate people seen as the other, as the antithesis to the perceived goodness of whiteness. This racist belief allowed white men to justify the enslavement and subsequent incarceration of Black Americans and the seizure of more than one billion acres of land from indigenous Americans from Independence Day in 1776 to 1887 alone.[4] White supremacy created the economic system that mothered every oppressive institution in America, including its most violent, the prison-industrial complex. To work toward the liberated and resurrected church Copeland describes, Catholics must become abolitionists.

---

3. Ibid., 35.

4. Claudio Saunt, *Unworthy Republic: The Dispossession of Native Americans and the Road to Indian Territory* (New York: W. W. Norton, 2020), 238. See also "Invasion of America," http://usg.maps.arcgis.com/apps/webappviewer/index.html?id=eb6ca76e008543a89349ff25 17db47e6#0.

Prison Models in the United States

The twentieth-century expansion of American jails and prisons was backed financially by private American corporations in industries such as health care, construction, and food. The first jail was created on July 27, 1776, just twenty-three days after the colonies declared independence from England. The first state penitentiary in America was created in 1790, when parts of the Pennsylvania Walnut Street jail were turned into housing for convicts. Incarcerated citizens ate, lived, and congregated together. Often, because many early prison reformers were Christian, the incarcerated, if they were able to read, were told to reflect and read Scripture. This Pennsylvania prison system promoted Christianity as a praxis for rehabilitation.

A second prison model, which was born out of Auburn, New York, eventually became the system used all over Europe and America in the twentieth century. Like the Pennsylvania model, the Auburn model was centered on solitude, silence, and isolation, but promoted the importance of the imprisoned laboring together. In this system, prisoners were not allowed to talk while working because reformers believed that silence improved efficiency.

Angela Davis identifies the European men who helped shape these systems, including John Howard, a Protestant philanthropist, and Jeremy Bentham, a philosopher.[5] These men, both English, believed that prisons and jails should be improved rather than eliminated. Howard believed that isolation from the rest of society could allow citizens the opportunity for religious introspection. Bentham argued that prisoners needed to labor, while being watched, in order to be truly rehabilitated and productive members of any given society. Davis describes

---

5. Davis, *Are Prisons Obsolete?*, 40–59.

Bentham's model, one of the first instances of surveillance in prisons, as a panopticon:

> Prisoners were to be housed in single cells on circular tiers, all facing a multilevel guard tower. By means of blinds and a complicated play of light and darkness, the prisoners—who would not see each other at all—would be unable to see the warden. From his vantage point, on the other hand, the warden would be able to see all of the prisoners. However—and this was the most significant aspect of Bentham's mammoth panopticon—because each individual prisoner would never be able to determine where the warden's gaze was focused, each prisoner would be compelled to act, that is, work, as if he were being watched at all times.[6]

By depriving these men of their human rights, reformers believed they were giving them not just the opportunity to self-reflect but to study Christianity. These reforms, many believed, would create a better and safer society. Following the Civil War and the passage of the Thirteenth Amendment, which prohibited slavery "except as a punishment for crime whereof the party shall have been duly convicted,"[7] local law enforcement, along with white supremacist organizations such as the Ku Klux Klan, arrested free Black women and men. These free citizens were incarcerated in Southern prisons and, in turn, were leased to private companies, including plantation owners. Many scholars describe this system as more inhumane than slavery. "Slave

---

6. Ibid., 46.

7. "Thirteenth Amendment," Abolition of Slavery Passed by Congress January 31, 1865. Ratified December 6, 1865. The Thirteenth Amendment changed a portion of article IV, section 2, https://constitutioncenter.org.

owners may have been concerned for the survival of individual slaves, who, after all, represented significant investments," writes Angela Davis. "Convicts, on the other hand, were leased not as individuals, but as a group, and they could be worked literally to death without affecting the profitability of a convict crew."[8] Davis notes that while both men and women were incarcerated post-Reconstruction, men were perceived as more redeemable than incarcerated women. Reformers viewed this merely as an opportunity to create facilities specifically designated to imprison and oppress women. The first prison for women was opened in Indiana in 1853. These prisons, originally called "reformatories," were segregated; and Black and indigenous women were not allowed to take part in the spaces meant to domesticate female prisoners.[9] Often women of color were forced to serve in the same leasing system that was exploiting Black men. As Davis writes, "Black women endured the cruelties of the convict lease system unmitigated by the feminization of punishment; neither their sentences nor the labor they were compelled to do were lessened by virtue of their gender."[10]

In 1934, Congress created the Federal Prison Industries (FPI) to help the incarcerated "acquire the work skills necessary to successfully make the transition from prison to law-abiding, contributing members of society."[11] The U.S. government owns the organization, which currently goes by the trade name UNICOR. Under federal law, every inmate in a federal prison is required to work; and under the Federal Prison Industries, incarcerated women and men make from 23 cents to $1.15 an

---

8. Davis, *Are Prisons Obsolete?*, 32.

9. See ibid., 72.

10. Ibid., 76.

11. "Federal Bureau of Prisons," https://www.bop.gov/about/history/timeline.jsp.

hour. According to the FPI website, the majority of the revenue it earns goes toward purchasing items from private-sector vendors; less than 25 percent for the salaries of staff; and just 5 percent for inmate wages. In 2019, the FPI net revenue was more than $500 million.[12] Less than a hundred years since the creation of the FPI, the federal and state prison population grew to 1,458,173. More than 200,000 American citizens are incarcerated in private prisons, which make more than five billion dollars a year. Comparatively, the prison population in the 1940s was just under twenty-five thousand. As of 2020, there are more than two million people incarcerated across the country in prisons, juvenile detention centers, jails, immigration detention, Indian country jails, psychiatric facilities, and military prisons.[13] Sixty percent of women in jails have not been convicted, and young Black girls make up 35 percent of the juvenile detention population. Transgender women and men, especially those who are Black and cannot pass, face higher rates of violence, including sexual assault, than the rest of the prison population.[14] At least 40 percent of incarcerated citizens who identify as transgender have been sexually assaulted. The prison-industrial complex, like chattel slavery, is a system designed to protect the interests of white men and women across the political spectrum from Donald Trump to Hillary Clinton.

Since the creation of the first jails and prisons, the prison-industrial complex—America's strongest economic industry since chattel slavery—has always been protected and served

---

12. "UNICOR," https://www.unicor.gov/FAQ_General.aspx.

13. "Prison Policy Initiative," https://www.prisonpolicy.org/reports/pie2019women.html.

14. National Center for Transgender Equality, *LGBTQ People Behind Bars: A Guide to Understanding the Issues Facing Transgender Prisoners and Their Legal Rights* (Washington, DC: NCTE, 2018), https://transequality.org/transpeoplebehindbars.

by U.S. law enforcement. According to Critical Resistance, the prison-industrial complex "is a term we use to describe the overlapping interests of government and industry that use surveillance, policing, and imprisonment as solutions to economic, social and political problems."[15] Policing enables the exploitation, torture, and slave labor of the prison system by violently harassing and targeting already marginalized communities, particularly Black women and men.

A world without prisons also means a world with police.

The Case for Abolition

What role does our Catholic identity play in the abolitionist movement? I was inspired by Catholic thinkers and organizations who were writing and talking about their faith and what it means to defund the police and abolish prisons and by individuals who used Catholic social teaching to discuss the gospel's call to be Catholic abolitionists. Dwayne David Paul, a friend and director of the Collaborative Center for Justice, a Catholic nonprofit organization based in Connecticut, described the role Catholics must play in abolishing police. Paul wrote about the role our faith can play in the struggle toward abolition. In June 2020, he wrote a piece that included demands about policing and action items that Catholics could follow. He called for banning the use of military equipment by U.S. police departments; prohibiting officers from taking part in military exercises; making no-knock warrants illegal; reducing funds allocated to law enforcement; and removing the certification of officers who are accused of any kind of misconduct.[16] In an article for the *Hartford Courant*, Paul and Rachel Lea Scott wrote, "We must

---

15. "Critical Resistance," http://criticalresistance.org.
16. Dwayne Paul, "Decriminalize Poverty to Reduce Police

shrink the scope of policework and the resources to do it. Those resources should be redirected to addressing the root causes of those problems rather than punishing the people who experience them."[17]

Thinkers such as Paul challenged me to think about my own role in abolition work. In July 2020, I took an online course focused on defunding the police. The panelists discussed policing as an institution that has been empowered by white supremacy and legal practices in our country, from the slave codes to present-day laws that criminalize poverty, mental health issues, and domestic abuse. Law enforcement helped in introducing enslavement's very horrors into the daily, twenty-first-century lives of Black Americans and other marginalized communities. Policing, the instructors taught, is merely another way to protect white supremacy and racial capitalism because they protect the very interests of those behind society's most oppressive spaces. Police officers, they proclaimed, serve as agents used to traumatize Black and Brown communities across the country.

Every day, the course began with each participant identifying the indigenous land they were currently residing on. I was living in an area of the Bronx that belonged to Lenape and Wappinger peoples. It was important to remind us of our nation's true origins, the panelists described, because it showed that law enforcement was just following the trauma that America has always caused. Violent policing can be traced from the early days of America, when indigenous peoples lost their lives and lands, to the twenty-first-century violence against antiracist

---

Violence," Collaborative Center for Justice, June 26, 2020, https://ccfj.org.

17. Dwayne David Paul and Rachel Lea Scott, "It's time to reclaim our communities from abusive policing," *Hartford Courant*, June 12, 2020, https://www.courant.com.

protestors. The panel, which included organizers from Dream Defenders,[18] an abolitionist group founded in 2012, and the Sunrise Movement, a climate change advocacy organization founded in 2017,[19] wanted participants to remember a time before capitalism, before slavery, before the European colonialism of the Americas. There was a time when life on these lands was truly liberated, when Brown, indigenous bodies lived free and sustainably. To strive toward a similarly liberated world, we must struggle toward a world where there is no prison-industrial complex exploiting and traumatizing vulnerable communities.

The fallacies and lies I had internalized about law enforcement and prisons were becoming apparent. These were not, despite the purported claims of early and contemporary Christian reformers, humane institutions that solved crime and kept our cities safe. The rapid militarization and tremendous state budgets given to police departments across America are justified because, according to pro-police supporters, police officers need resources to battle crime. However, almost half of police interactions with lay Americans over the age of sixteen involved traffic stops. According to abolitionist Mariame Kaba, police officers, at most, solve one felony a year.[20]

As noted earlier, since the earliest days of slave patrols and the creation of the first American police departments, white men, with the backing of an emerging racially capitalist system and an established white supremacist government, stole more than one billion acres of land from indigenous Americans. White men believed that it was their destiny and God-given right as Christians to take possession of land and exploit Black and

---

18. Dream Defenders, https://dreamdefenders.org.

19. Sunrise Movement, https://www.sunrisemovement.org.

20. Mariame Kaba, "Yes, We Mean Literally Abolish the Police," *New York Times*, June 12, 2020, https://www.nytimes.com.

indigenous citizens. White men were not just exceptional; they had a right to dominate. White Americans have internalized this idea since the first colonizers arrived. Not only did white people have a right to control, exploit, and kill other cultures, they were also superior to all other citizens, especially Black Americans. The United States of America, from education to prisons to politics, has internalized the very white supremacy its leaders claim to reject. White men have always regarded themselves as the arbiters of freedom—who gets to have it and who does not. Abolition, I was realizing, is the only way to rid our nation and world of the white supremacy to which it has always clung. As Kaba writes, "When you see a police officer pressing his knee into a black man's neck until he dies, that's the logical result of policing in America. When a police officer brutalizes a black person, he is doing what he sees as his job."[21]

The year 2020 made me, and countless other Catholics, realize how pivotal it was for our church to get involved in abolition. For the first time, I realized that this system did not care to save the lives of my people, or countless white Americans for that matter; people died during a global pandemic and the Trump administration continued to demonstrate how little regard it had for human life. Along with Blacks and Latinos dying during the pandemic, the effects of racial capitalism were also seen in the violence and murder happening across the nation, including the violent xenophobic attacks against the Asian American community.[22] Transgender women and men, too, were being attacked; as we have noted, at least twenty transgender people

---

21. Ibid.

22. Neil G. Ruiz, Juliana Menasce Horowitz, and Christine Tamir, "Many Black and Asian Americans Say They Have Experienced Discrimination amid the COVID-19 Outbreak," Pew Research Center, July 1, 2020, https://www.pewsocialtrends.org.

were killed in the first half of 2020 alone.[23] In June, the Trump administration passed legislation that allowed employers to fire someone who was gay, lesbian, or transgender; this was eventually struck down by the Supreme Court. In September, the president, following the death of Justice Ruth Bader Ginsburg, nominated Amy Coney Barrett, a conservative Catholic, to replace the vacant seat on the Supreme Court; many Americans fear that Barrett will roll back legal advances that protect those in the LGBTQIA community. In the media, intellectuals, who decried threats to human dignity and liberties, published a piece in *Harper's Magazine* titled, "A Letter on Justice and Open Debate" that openly promoted the very culture that was killing Black transgender women and men across the country. Note, for example, Gabrielle Bellot, a transgender Black woman, who wrote that those with privilege, resources, and a large platform wanted "the freedom for people to ask whether or not freaks like me should be allowed to transition, should be allowed in the women's restroom, should be allowed not to suffer the overwhelming pain of gender dysphoria?"[24]

As the secular world seemed to grow more and more violent, the Catholic Church's leaders continued to miss the mark on their various public statements. Despite the *Zeitgeist* focusing on abolition and what it means to adopt reformist versus abolitionist practices, the U.S. bishops were publishing statements that ignored the real violence of our world in favor of romanticized notions of American law enforcement as beacons of justice that

---

23. Human Rights Campaign, "Violence against the Transgender and Gender Non-Conforming Community in 2020," https://www.hrc.org.

24. Gabrielle Bellot, "Freedom Means *Can* Rather Than *Should*: What the *Harper's* Open Letter Gets Wrong," Literary Hub, July 8, 2020, https://lithub.com.

deserved not just our undying loyalty as Christians but unquestioned power backed by our tax dollars. Collectively, the bishops ignored the topics Catholics most wanted them to address, while individual clergy continued to show their white supremacist Christianity, including a pastor, who compared Black organizers to maggots.[25]

During the online abolition course, participants were asked to describe true liberation in their own words. Answers included freedom from white supremacy; more green spaces for children from vulnerable communities; no police brutality; no more murders of Black transgender women and men. Abolition is the key to a world free of violence and oppression; and in order to achieve it, we need to shift society from one that relies on the prison-industrial complex to one that is committed to using radical approaches to eradicate social ills that cause incarceration, including addiction, homelessness, mental health problems, and housing. To work toward such liberation, toward resurrection, our church must be committed to an abolitionist-centered transformative justice.

Transformative Justice

In 2016, I interviewed Lucy McBath, the mother of Jordan Davis. McBath helped me to appreciate the role of the resurrection in Christian organizing. On November 23, 2012, her son was out with three friends; and, while at a gas station in Jacksonville, Florida, the teenagers were approached by a forty-five-year-old white man named Michael Dunn. He demanded they lower their music; and when they refused, he shot into the

---

25. Katherine Fung, "Catholic Church Pastor Compares Black Lives Matter Protesters to 'Maggots and Parasites,'" *Newsweek*, June 30, 2020, https://www.newsweek.com.

vehicle, shooting Davis in the neck, legs, and lungs. After the teenager's death, Dunn, who killed Davis with a gun he legally possessed, was charged with first-degree murder. He is currently serving a ninety-year prison sentence.

I was introduced to McBath through a college friend, Valerie Jean-Charles, a brilliant, Haitian-American writer, who, at the time, worked with Everytown for Gun Safety, a nonprofit gun reform advocacy group. McBath told me that it was her faith that ultimately helped her survive her son's murder. Months after Davis's death, her sister told her about a conversation she had with him before his death. The young man told his aunt, "I want to thank you because God has shown me how much you pray for me. And I want you to know that I'm going to be okay and that one day, everyone will know who I am." She described how her son knew that his life, while short, would help her fight for a more just world, one where white men were not allowed to possess weapons for murdering Black children. Knowing this gave McBath purpose. She realized that God was calling her to fight against the very policies that led to Davis's death. This purpose, she told me, is "the reason why, today, I am not devastated, by any means, over Jordan's death. I am happy for him because that's where I want to be, too. As a parent of faith, that's what you want for your children," she said. "To know that my child is with the Father, to know that my child gets to glorify God every moment for all of eternity makes me very grateful. I'm very grateful to God that Jordan is with him." McBath was forced to grapple with America's relationship with guns following the death of Trayvon Martin, another Black teenager murdered just nine months before her own son. Martin's death made her acknowledge her own privilege in being, at the time, so removed from violence. After her own tragedy, she became familiar with gun policies and reform efforts and began to publicly share her story. She was the national spokesperson for Moms Demand Action for Gun Sense in America and served as the outreach leader for Everytown for Gun Safety. In 2018, she successfully ran for Congress and became U.S. representative for Georgia's Sixth Congressional District. She described her work as a way to continue to honor the memory of her son.

As Christians, McBath told me, we are accountable to one another as a faith community, and we need to push one another to organize and fight for justice toward a truly resurrected, Christ-centered world. Like Copeland, McBath understood that death was not the final word; even in the most horrific moments of white violence, death and white supremacy would not reign over McBath and the legacy of her son. Her witness and vocation demonstrated the power, and the paradox, as Copeland noted, of God's love, one that was always centered in the struggle toward "the unexpected, unimagined resurrection," one that "interrupts, reveals, and projects justice, mercy, and love into the bleakest circumstances."[26] Toward the end of our 2016 conversation, she told me that, on a trip to New York, she stepped into St. Patrick's Cathedral and found herself grappling with the truth that God had revealed to her: that she must forgive her son's killer. She sobbed in the church for over an hour; and when she walked out of the church, she had forgiven Dunn. "Part of truly trying to walk out as a Christian is love, acceptance, and forgiveness," she concluded. McBath, like Tarana Burke, represented the diverse, Black experiences that our church must center and learn from. A world free of violence required transformative justice as a strategy toward a world without the need for prisons and policing.

Transformative justice is the process toward a society free of policing as a way to respond to violence and other harms. This

---

26. Copeland, *Knowing Christ Crucified*, 36.

is a radical approach that demands that we collectively reexamine the ways that we talk about crime, mental health, violence, and gender. It means reshifting the narrative of police as moral arbiters of justice, when, in fact, police departments have been direct extensions of chattel slavery. These departments learned from a system that exploited and sold Black citizens. Black bodies, our nation has always taught, were to be feared, possessed, and discarded whenever it was deemed necessary. Violence has existed since this nation's birth, but policing was not its solution; police officers were merely brutal enforcers. Institutions that oppress vulnerable and marginalized communities always created the very social conditions that led to crime across the United States, including poverty, underfunded schools, and lack of housing. If we care about creating a world in which *all*—not just white Americans—are to thrive, we need to create a world that is free of policing. Transformative justice provides the rhetoric and tools to work toward abolition. In *Beyond Survival*, the writers state that this restorative process is necessary "to prevent violence, to intervene when harm is occurring, to hold people accountable, and to transform individuals and society to build safer communities." In other words, communities work together to address the issues they are facing as marginalized individuals, including the violence they face at the hands of abusers or the police, create networks to support survivors and victims of abuse; and, in turn, survivors help to educate their respective communities on how best to work toward justice and the elimination of violence.[27]

If abolition means a liberated world, one centered on the fight for justice, then what role do Catholics play in twenty-first-century abolition? As I noted earlier, the bishops, as part of

27. Dixon and Piepzna-Samarasinha (eds.), *Beyond Survival*, chapter 1.

their own accountability process, must work to actively engage and learn from the work of women such as Mariame Kaba and Angela Davis. As they gather, bishops must also, whenever possible, invite these leaders to educate them at their national gatherings. They must be willing to encounter and learn from Black women outside of the church, as they did when they hosted social-justice activist Bryan Stephenson. The church must also campaign for defunding and demilitarizing law enforcement. The bishops must engage with the abolitionist discussions currently happening in our nation. An abolitionist framework is one that aligns not just with our Catholic faith but also with the guidance of Pope Francis.

In 2019, the pope was critical of the "throwaway culture" that allocates millions of dollars and countless resources "to repress offenders instead of truly seeking to promote the integral development of people, which reduces the circumstances that favor committing illegal acts."[28] Francis, unfortunately, lacks the expertise and understanding of the history of prisons and policing to make demands beyond a reformist, instead of an abolitionist, lens; however, in the context of the Catholic Church, his words serve as a launching pad for bishops, who must, at bare minimum, demand the drastic defunding of law enforcement, the demilitarization of U.S. police officers; and a reallocation into, as Francis describes, "resources to address the social, psychological and family problems experienced by detainees."

Therefore, our bishops must, first, call for governments across

---

28. Pope Francis, Speech to Participants at the International Meeting for Regional and National Managers of Prison Pastoral Care, November 8, 2019, as reported by Cindy Wooden, "Concern for Inmates, Prison Reform Is Obligatory Act of Mercy, Pope Says," *National Catholic Reporter*, November 8, 2019, https://www.ncronline. org.

the country to defund the police and demand that resources be placed into charities that are working to eradicate poverty, homelessness, domestic abuse, and addiction, including those sponsored by the church, and allocate resources to support organizations that can help to mediate violence and work to interrupt the need for 911 emergencies.

Second, bishops must be willing to learn from contemporary abolitionists such as Derecka Purnell. She is a writer, human rights lawyer, and organizer. In 2019, she spoke alongside Angela Davis at the Riverside Church. Purnell described her first time organizing a rally following the murder of Trayvon Martin. She credited Charlene Carruthers, a Black, queer feminist and one of the creators of the Black Youth Project 100, a Black youth advocacy group founded in 2013 following the acquittal of George Zimmerman, with teaching her how to organize. Carruthers taught her to think critically about what it means to organize. After college, Purnell attended Harvard Law School, where she found guidance in the scholarship of women such as Davis.

In 2020, Purnell wrote about her journey to becoming an abolitionist.[29] She was not always an abolitionist, so she understood firsthand why people were apprehensive; however, she was evidence that a shift toward an abolitionist politic was possible. Purnell discussed her learning experience and created a guidance plan for people who were new to abolition. She wanted readers to understand that abolition, like all movements for Black liberation, welcomed people who were committed to eradicating oppression and white supremacy. Abolition, Purnell wrote, created a space where we were all welcomed and encouraged to reimagine and work for a better, safer world, where violence and inequality were not the norm. This was a society we,

---

29. Derecka Purnell, "How I Became a Police Abolitionist," *The Atlantic*, July 6, 2020, https://www.theatlantic.com.

as Catholics, find in the resurrection. There was hope because it was not the end; rather, a transformation into something better, holier. U.S. bishops must explicitly commit to Black liberation, including but not limited to embracing the Black Lives Matter movement and encouraging Catholics to consider adopting an abolitionist lens.

Immediate steps that the church can also take in the struggle toward transformative liberation include, first, creating a website for the Ad Hoc Committee Against Racism (ACAR) so that Catholics can see the ongoing work of the USCCB's antiracism group. Currently, it seems as if the ACAR has not done anything since its 2018 pastoral letter. Second, Pope Francis should call for and attend a gathering in the United States to encourage bishops to address the issue of race. If he is going to be so adamant about unity, then this must begin with the bishops he has selected to help run the U.S. church.[30] Third, dioceses across the country must develop antiracism training for all clergy in formation, especially white priests to understand systemic oppression more fully.

The Black Lives Matter Movement

Racial capitalism has robbed my family, like it has many others, since our arrival in the United States. My paternal cousin, Miguelito, was two years younger than me. His father arrived in the United States shortly after my parents. Several years later, my mother and father would bring his wife and my cousin to the United States. When Miguelito was a teenager, he was in a car crash, from which he was recovering for years. An adolescent

---

30. Junno Arocho Esteves, "U.S. Catholic Media Must Inspire Unity amid Division, Pope Says," *Catholic News Service*, June 30, 2020, https://www.americamagazine.org.

at the time of his accident, his mind deteriorated soon after. He was angry and lost; and the solution, according to doctors, was simply medication and time. In February 2017, he committed suicide outside the front door of his family home. His father discovered his body in the early morning hours. Several days after his death, I traveled with my family for his wake and funeral, on February 21, in Florida. I remembered him smiling the last time we spoke. There had been distance between us, years since we'd last seen one another. This was the distance of families, the one that occurs when immigrants in the United States make the often-predictable shift down south, away from the rough, make-or-break streets of New York City. (His family migrated to Florida when I was sixteen.) Aside from conversations—phone calls here and there—we had not really stayed in touch. Yet here I was, standing in solidarity with his parents and his sister. I watched and marveled at his sister's beauty and stoicism. No tears fell from her eyes; unlike her parents, she stood tall, ironically a source of strength.

I never saw my father pray before. But there he stood, arms wrapped around his brother, as he joined in the pastor's call to prayer. I do not know the words he uttered, but I cried as I watched him. I was struggling to see God in this moment—and all of the moments that weekend—and my father's moment of prayer unraveled me. All weekend, I had been struggling to understand where God was. *If God loved us, why was there so much pain, so much heartbreak and suffering in our communities?* And yet, there he was, in the quiet embrace between two brothers, I saw God. It took me years to understand my cousin's death and the ways in which the system failed to truly help him heal following his accident; often, I wondered what his life could have been in a world where mental health problems were treated, and where Black kids were given the resources to heal and survive. Copeland's theology stated that this tragedy was not the end. We were to remember the pain but not fear it—for resurrection and liberation, her work demonstrated, require us to fight to eradicate the very ills most affecting our communities, from addiction to poverty to suicide.

A world without these ills is a world without prisons, without police, without the very systems responsible for violence and inequity. The Catholic Church has a crucial role to play in the struggle for liberation. Along with the aforementioned action items, the United States bishops must appoint a Black liberation consultant who can liaise between the church and various organizers involved in the fight for Black liberation. This will help American bishops to understand the issues communities of color are most concerned with outside of just the issues they believe matter to us.

Finally, bishops must give women like Garza, Cullors, and Tometi the same space they have given people like Bryan Stephenson and Abby Johnson. Following the release of a film by the latter, the bishops published a statement that referenced Johnson's work and listed key factors Catholics must remember about abortion. Despite Johnson's racist comments during the antiracism protests of 2020, the church did not condemn the statements of a woman they have repeatedly referenced, nor did they release any statement engaging with the work of Black organizers who uphold the Christian tenets dear to our faith. I want my church and leaders to be committed to saving and uplifting Black lives. Black women have given us the blueprint for freedom. Let's become a truly liberated and resurrected church.

Index

of Black Lives Matter movement, 23–37
Black transgender, violence
against, 15
incarceration of, 115
and U.S. Catholic Church,
22
women of color
in American prisons, 115,
116
reaction to COVID-19 pan-
demic, 108

Woodard, Sergeant Isaac, 42
Woodson, Jacqueline, 42
Working Group on Slavery,
Memory, and Reconcilia-
tion (Georgetown Univer-
sity), 46, 47

Zaher, Dounya, 9
Zimmerman, George, 2, 3, 27,
89, 127